Crosscurrents / MODERN CRITIQUES

Harry T. Moore, *General Editor*

Moment of Torment

An Interpretation of Franz Kafka's Short Stories

Ruth Tiefenbrun

WITH A PREFACE BY

Harry T. Moore

SOUTHERN ILLINOIS UNIVERSITY PRESS
Carbondale and Edwardsville

FEFFER & SIMONS, INC.
London and Amsterdam

For Joe

Library of Congress Cataloging in Publication Data

Tiefenbrun, Ruth, 1904–
  Moment of torment.

  Bibliography: p.
  1. Kafka, Franz, 1883–1924. 2. Homosexuality and
literature. I. Title.
PT2621.A26Z936   833'.9'12   72–8911
ISBN 0–8093–0620–4

Contents

Contents

Preface

In the nearly forty-one years of his existence until June 1924, Franz Kafka published little. After his death, his friend, literary executor, and biographer-to-be, Max Brod, fortunately didn't carry out Kafka's written instructions to burn all his remaining manuscripts and any of his letters which could be found, as well as stories which had been printed in newspapers and magazines. Brod in the 1920s supervised the publication of his friend's three novels and the many stories he left in manuscript.

Most of these works appeared in English in the 1930s, translated from the German by Edwin and Willa Muir. In 1948, Kafka's Diaries, dating from 1910 and 1923, came out in an English translation. There were also letters and numerous books about him, among which we have the present volume by Ruth Tiefenbrun. Kafka now ranks, and rightly so, among the greatest twentieth-century writers of fiction.

But even the most favorable responses to his work have differed. Critics have called it primarily theological, fantastic, grotesque, existential, metaphysical, or just plain literary-symbolist. Mrs. Tiefenbrun's book will probably give the earlier commentators something of a jolt. Even those who disagree most vehemently with her findings will have to read her book to judge its presentation of evidence.

Kafka's complications lie not only in his family life,

but also in the city in which he was born and in which he lived after growing up. There is no city in the Western world quite comparable to Prague (and I have seen all those which count). Prague is one of those "special" cities like Venice, Budapest, Copenhagen, or Amsterdam. But Prague, with its twisting little streets, has a unique intermixture of Gothic and Baroque in the towers and domes that crowd its skyline. (Those who have not seen Prague will find that the photographic illustrations of two books help to project the atmosphere of the place in relation to Kafka: Pavel Eisner's Franz Kafka and Prague, 1951, with pictures by Karel Plicka and others; and Emanuel Frynta's Kafka and Prague, 1960, with camera work by Jan Lukas.)

In Kafka's youth, the bureaucracy of the Austro-Hungarian Empire flourished, and he seems, among other things, to be satirizing that bureaucracy in some of his stories and in his novels The Castle and The Trial. Today there is a Soviet-imposed bureaucracy, as well as "social-realist" ideals in the arts. For many years in the Eastern European countries Kafka was anathema to those who knew of him; many didn't. At the Jewish Cemetery in Prague in 1960, I asked an attendant whether Kafka were buried there, and he told me he had never heard of him. I knew from Max Brod's biography that Kafka had died in a sanatorium near Vienna and, after visiting Prague, I learned that he had been interred in a suburban graveyard with his parents. Frynta's Kafka and Prague has a picture of the headstone. I have also learned why he was condemned by the "social realists" in Stalin's time: he represented what they called bourgeois decadence; the characters in his fiction were maladjusted. But the author of "In The Penal Colony," a powerful story anticipating the Nazi concentration camps, was rescued from both anathema and oblivion when a Kafka Conference celebrated the eightieth anniversary of his birth, in 1963, at Libice, near Prague. He has survived even the abortive Czech revolt of 1968; his books are printed and read in Eastern Europe.

That previously mentioned headstone in the suburban Jewish cemetery has three names on it: Dr. Franz Kafka is at the top; his father, Hermann, is immediately beneath, with his mother, Julie, below. The title of doctor was earned in the law school of the Karl-Ferdinand University in Prague. But Kafka, following the customary post-graduate year he spent in the courts, didn't go on to practice law. He became a part of the government bureaucracy, employed by the Workers' Accident Institute for the kingdom of Bohemia. Max Brod noted that "Whole chapters of the novels The Trial and The Castle derive their outer covers, their realistic wrappings, from the atmosphere Kafka breathed in the Workers' Accident Institute."

As for his father, Hermann Kafka, he was the subject (really the object) of one of his son's most notable pieces of writing, a letter to him. Franz Kafka gave this letter to his mother, to pass on to the father, but she instead kept this remarkable document, a statement of the son's lifelong feeling of helplessness before his forceful-merchant male parent with his self-assured and loud-voiced, bustling personality. Mrs. Tiefenbrun uses this letter as part of her case.

Several women played important parts in Kafka's life. The first of them was long known as a mysterious figure, "Fräulein F.B." Kafka became engaged to her in 1914, but two years later broke away from the attachment. They became betrothed again in 1917, but before the year was out he once more drew away. The girl, who we now know was named Felice Bauer, then married someone else. In 1919–20, Kafka was engaged to Julie Wohryzec, but gave her up when he met Milena Jesenská, recipient of the Letters to Milena, first published in 1952. On page 24 of the present book, Mrs. Tiefenbrun discusses this relationship and what it meant to Kafka. In 1923, he formed still another attachment, this time with a Jewish girl named Dora Dymant, with whom he lived in Berlin and Prague. Before he died the following year, he wanted to marry Dora, but her family's rabbi refused

to perform the service because Kafka had drifted away
from orthodoxy. As Mrs. Tiefenbrun points out, his relationship with Dora enabled him for the first time to
overcome his father's spell upon him. Although he was
fatally ill with tuberculosis, this was the happiest time
of his life. As Mrs. Tiefenbrun says, he had at last
achieved a "psychosexual balance." She also notes that,
"for the first time he desperately wanted to live and
followed his doctor's orders 'with exactitude' and without protest." But it was too late, and he died at the
Kierling Sanatorium in Austria on June 3, 1924. I have
already briefly traced his posthumous emergence as an
outstanding twentieth-century author.

In the light of Mrs. Tiefenbrun's thesis about Kafka,
we may find it interesting to consider a few other writers
who have turned out what might be called psychoanalytic biographies of revered authors. One of them is
Rebecca Peterson, whose The Riddle of Emily Dickinson (1951), appeared under the imprint of an ancient
and respectable publishing firm, Houghton Mifflin. The
jacket of the book confidently stated, "Now the ninety-
year-old mystery is ended, the dialogue completed." But
not as far as some horrified reviewers were concerned:
Mrs. Peterson's attempt to show that the chief passion
of Emily Dickinson's life was a lesbian attachment came
as a violent shock; one discussion of the book complained that the author even provided us "a bedroom
scene" as part of her argument.

Another biography that created an uproar in the 1950s
was Richard Aldington's book on Lawrence of Arabia.
This touched the patriotism of many Englishmen, and
Aldington was vituperated for pointing out that a popu-
lar hero was a homosexual as well as a fraud. The "other
Lawrence"—D. H.—was also recently put under close
scrutiny in a book by Emile Delavenay entitled D. H.
Lawrence and Edward Carpenter. With very good reason for believing so, he launched a hypothesis to the
effect that this Lawrence had been influenced by Carpenter's sexual philosophy. Since Carpenter was a friend
of people Lawrence knew in the town where he was

born, and who owned copies of his books, it seems possible that Lawrence at least was familiar with Carpenter's theories, even if he never met him; but so far no direct evidence in the matter has turned up. Yet, as John Lehmann observed in the Sunday Telegraph (London), Professor Delavenay "has made an almost totally convincing case for [Lawrence's] having read Carpenter's work." There is also Phyllis Greenacre's Swift and Carroll: A Psychoanalytic Study of Two Lives (1955), a book which analyzed the authors of, respectively, Gulliver's Travels and Alice in Wonderland, showing how they were attracted to what Vladimir Nabakov has so neatly called nymphets. In the course of her book, Dr. Greenacre mentioned a paper, read by Dr. Paul Shilder before a group of psychoanalysts in 1936, which dealt with some of the problems of Alice in Wonderland. Dr. Schilder was violently attacked by "the outraged protectors of Alice." Dr. Greenacre's own book didn't seem to draw that kind of fire in 1951, perhaps because the jacket identified her as, among much else, a Professor of Clinical Psychology at Cornell University.

In college, Mrs. Tiefenbrun majored in Clinical Psychology and took her M.S. degree in Education. Her book is, like those just mentioned, built on hypothesis: she finds indications in Kafka's writing that show him to have been a homosexual. What kind of fire this is going to draw from Kafka admirers can only be a matter, at this stage, for guesswork; but perhaps the twentieth century is sufficiently advanced to enable us to receive such matters with a certain calmness. In 1971, when Professor Delavenay's book came out in England and America, it wasn't assaulted by Lawrenceans. In her study, Mrs. Tiefenbrun is not condemning Kafka, but rather merely attempting to investigate the meaning of his work. The least that can be said now is that this volume will interest all serious readers of Kafka.

HARRY T. MOORE

Southern Illinois University
September 11, 1972

Acknowledgments

Quotations reprinted by permission of Schocken Books Inc. from *The Penal Colony* by Franz Kafka, copyright © 1948 by Schocken Books Inc.; from *The Great Wall of China* by Franz Kafka, copyright © 1948 by Schocken Books Inc. (published in England under the title *Description of a Struggle and The Great Wall of China*); from *The Diaries of Franz Kafka 1910–1913*, copyright © 1948 by Schocken Books Inc.; from *The Diaries of Franz Kafka 1914–1923*, copyright © 1949 by Schocken Books Inc.; from *Dearest Father* by Franz Kafka, copyright © 1954 by Schocken Books Inc. (published in England under the title "Dearest Father" in *Wedding Preparations and Other Prose Writings*); from *Letters to Milena* by Franz Kafka, copyright © 1953 by Schocken Books Inc.; from *Description of a Struggle* by Franz Kafka, copyright © 1958 by Schocken Books Inc. (published in England under the title *Description of a Struggle and The Great Wall of China*); and from *Franz Kafka: A Biography* by Max Brod, copyright © 1947, 1960 by Schocken Books Inc.

Quotations reprinted by permission of Martin Secker and Warburg Limited from the following works of Franz Kafka: *The Trial*; *The Castle*; *Amerika*; the *Diaries*, Vols. I and II; *In the Penal Colony*; *Letters to Milena*; *Description of a Struggle and The Great Wall of China*; and "Dearest Father" and other writings from *Wedding Preparations and Other Prose Writings*.

Quotations from *Franz Kafka: A Biography* by Max Brod, published by Martin Secker and Warburg Limited, reprinted by permission of A. M. Heath & Company Ltd. and Martin Secker and Warburg Limited.

Acknowledgment is extended to Random House Inc.–Alfred A. Knopf Inc. for permission to reprint from the following copyrighted works by Franz Kafka: *The Castle*, translated by Willa and Edwin Muir with additional materials translated by Eithne Wilkins and Ernst Kaiser, definitive edition published by Alfred A. Knopf, Inc., 1954; and *The Trial*, translated by Willa and Edwin Muir and E. M. Butler, definitive edition published by Alfred A. Knopf, Inc., 1957.

Quotations from: *Franz Kafka: A Critical Study of His Writings* by Wilhelm Emrich. Copyright © 1968 by Frederick Ungar Publishing Co., Inc. Reprinted by permission.

Reprinted from *Amerika* by Franz Kafka, translated by Edwin Muir. Copyright 1946 by New Directions Publishing Corporation. Reprinted by permission of New Directions Publishing Corporation. (Quotations appearing in this book are taken from the first Schocken Paperback edition, which lists Willa and Edwin Muir as translators, published in association with New Directions, 1962.)

Quotations from *Conversations with Kafka* by Gustav Janouch, translated by Goronwy Rees. Copyright © 1968, 1971 by Fischer Verlag GmbH., Frankfurt-am-Main. Reprinted by permission of New Directions Publishing Corporation.

Quotations from *Conversations with Kafka* by Gustav Janouch also by permission of André Deutsch Limited Publishers.

Quotations from *Sex and Morality*, copyright, 1954, by Abram Kardiner, reprinted by permission of the publisher, The Bobbs-Merrill Company, Inc.

Especial appreciation is extended to Calvin S. Hall, who read my manuscript several times. Despite differences of opinion which we discussed in a most amicable fashion, Calvin Hall gave me invaluable advice and suggestions which I incorporated and which contributed to the final shape of my book. I also wish to express my gratitude to Angel and Kate Flores who assisted me conscientiously with many questions of stylistic detail and also made many invaluable suggestions.

Key to Editions

A   *Amerika*. Translated by Edwin Muir. New York: New Directions, 1946, first Schocken Paperback edition (from which quotations appearing in this book were taken) published in association with New Directions, 1962.

B   *Franz Kafka: A Biography*. By Max Brod, translated by G. Humphreys Roberts and Richard Winston. Second edition. New York: Schocken Books, Inc., 1960.

C   *The Castle*. Translated by Willa and Edwin Muir with additional materials translated by Eithne Wilkins and Ernst Kaiser. Definitive edition. New York: Alfred A. Knopf, Inc., 1954.

CHRL   *Dreams, Life, and Literature: A Study of Franz Kafka*. By Calvin S. Hall and Richard E. Lind. Chapel Hill: University of North Carolina Press, 1970.

DF   *Dearest Father: Stories and Other Writings*. Translated by Ernst Kaiser and Eithne Wilkins. New York: Schocken Books, Inc., 1954.

DI   *The Diaries of Franz Kafka: 1910–1913*. Edited by Max Brod, translated by Joseph Kresh. New York: Schocken Books., 1948.

DII   *The Diaries of Franz Kafka: 1914–1923*. Edited by Max Brod, translated by Martin Greenberg and Hannah Arendt. New York: Schocken Books, Inc., 1949.

DS   *Description of a Struggle*. Translated by Tania and James Stern. New York: Schocken Books, Inc., 1958.

E   *Franz Kafka: A Critical Study of His Writings*. By Wilhelm Emrich, translated by Sheema Z.

Buehne. New York: Frederick Ungar Publishing Co., Inc., 1968.

FKHT   *Franz Kafka: An Interpretation of his Works.* By Herbert Tauber, translated by G. Humphreys Roberts and Roger Senhouse. New Haven: Yale University Press, 1948.

FKT   *Franz Kafka Today.* Angel Flores and Homer Swander, eds. Madison: University of Wisconsin Press, 1958.

GW   *The Great Wall of China.* Translated by Willa and Edwin Muir. New York: Schocken Books, Inc., 1948.

J   *Conversations with Kafka.* By Gustav Janouch, translated by Goronwy Rees. New York: New Directions, ND Paperback, 1971.

M   *Letters to Milena.* Translated by Tania and James Stern. New York: Schocken Books, Inc., 1953.

P   *Franz Kafka: Parable and Paradox.* By Heinz Politzer. Revised and expanded edition. Ithaca, N. Y.: Cornell University Press, Cornell Paperbacks, 1966.

PC   *The Penal Colony.* Translated by Willa and Edwin Muir. New York: Schocken Books, Inc., 1948.

SAM   *Sex and Morality.* By Abram Kardiner. Indianapolis: The Bobbs-Merrill Company, Inc., 1954.

T   *The Trial.* Translated by Willa and Edwin Muir and E. M. Butler. Definitive edition. New York: Alfred A. Knopf, Inc., 1957.

TKP   *The Kafka Problem.* Angel Flores, ed. New York: New Directions, 1946.

1

Moment of Torment

Kafka, the most inscrutable, enigmatic, and incomprehensible of all writers, harped obsessively on one theme—
the plight of a man who has suddenly been propelled out
of the protective sheath of his routine living, who has
become an outcast, barred forever from marrying and
acquiring a progeny which would link him to the chain
of generations. The condition of this man is so intolerable that there is no solution for him but suicide. He is
dead while he is still alive. Because of some inexplicable
catastrophe, his life has become so incomprehensible
that every commonplace occurrence strikes him with
amazement. The most ordinary conversation seems to
him to be a miracle because all of life has become incredible. His world is in a state of dissolution in which "high
houses collapse every now and then for no apparent
reason" (DS, 63–64). All of humanity looks at him as
if he were a pariah or as if he had become dehumanized.
All civilization feels it has a right to torture him. All
authorities declare him guilty without a trial and execute
him without mentioning the reason for his execution.

Although Kafka's protagonists view the world with dis-
trust, recognizing the obsolescence of its laws, the disintegration of its moral judgments, the degradation of
its human values, and the indifferent brutality of its authority figures, Kafka's heroes spend their lives seeking
to open doors that will lead to their acceptance in this
worst of all possible worlds. Even though there is no

nourishment for them on earth so that they must starve to death, even though all of the satisfactions of ordinary men are barred to them, they struggle persistently to gain acceptance in this world as if it were a lost paradise.

There is never a rational explanation of why Kafka's characters find themselves in this terrible predicament. Thus, in "In the Penal Colony," the condemned prisoner does not know what commandment he has broken until he is at the point of death, when his transgression is pierced through his flesh by the harrow of the torture machine. He does not even know that he has been sentenced, nor has he had an opportunity to defend himself. In "The Metamorphosis," Kafka never explains why gentle, self-sacrificing Gregor is subjected to the catastrophes which descend upon him. No explicator has given a plausible reason for his dehumanization, alienation, persecution, and finally his death sentence. In *The Trial*, the first sentence reads: "Someone must have traduced Joseph K., for without having done anything wrong, he was arrested one fine morning." We hypothesize that if Kafka had chosen to divulge exactly what the slanderer had said, we would immediately know why the Court knew beyond question of doubt that Joseph K. was guilty, and why he became so disturbed when he was arrested that he immediately contemplated suicide. We would also know why Joseph K., who persevered so fanatically in trying to prove his innocence, dragged his executioners *away* from a policeman who seemed ready to come to his rescue, and rushed them to the place of his execution. We would recognize the paradoxical nature of the law in the case of the invisible Court against Joseph K.

Some of Kafka's explicators have conjectured that Kafka had a deep personal problem which he kept an inviolate secret. They knew of Kafka's father fixation and were aware that he considered sexual relationships with women filthy and obscene; therefore these problems could not have been his secret. Kate Flores notes that the startling and inexplicable features of "The Judgment" seem to be related to Kafka's secret and remarks: "perhaps all of Kafka's stories are infinitely subtle private analogies" (FKT, 16). She also observes: "From one point of view Kafka's life and work may be a long study in certain consequences upon the suppression of abnormal love" (FKT, 21). Heinz Politzer notes: "what was and remains his [Kafka's] problem becomes the secret of his heroes" (P, 46).

These explicators must have wondered why Kafka was so excessively evasive and secretive; why he invariably refrained from disclosing the explicit reason for his characters' torment; why he consistently made a mystery or a horror story of even his seemingly innocuous narratives. For example, "The Hunger Artist," which seems to be a straightforward story, ends in an ambiance of ominous mystery. In a dying whisper, the artist informs his dwindled audience of the overseer and his attendants that they must not admire him for his fasting. He tells them frankly that he could not tolerate the kind of food he could attain in this world. Had he been able to eat it, he "would have made no fuss and stuffed" himself "like you or anyone else," thereby implying that he would never have become a hunger artist. What was the unattainable nourishment that he was seeking? Politzer observes that the unattainable nourishment that Gregor was seeking was an incestuous relationship with his sister (P, 77). While discussing the concept of "unattainable nourishment" in "The Hunger Artist," Politzer comments that Kafka "never came to know the nourishment, the nurturing elements of his own existence" (P, 307). Could Kafka have meant many things by this concept? We do not think so. We believe that his enigmatic "food," "music," and "nourishment" images are consistent throughout the totality of his works.

Although Kafka thoroughly enjoyed reading his stories to his acquaintances and the members of his family, he was extremely secretive and evasive about the explicit meanings of any of his narratives. When queried about his stories, he always made some cryptic remark which

left his questioner completely baffled (J, 30–31). Nevertheless, he reiterated in his diaries, letters, and conversations that he wrote only about himself and for himself.
He told Milena that he was always unhappy when his
purely personal affairs were being published (M, 131);
he told Janouch that his narratives were "personal proofs"
of his "human weakness" (J, 26). Despite his reputation
for undeviating honesty, none of his friends seems to
have taken him seriously.

We are taking Kafka at his word in our interpretation
of his writings and believe that all of his major protagonists share his "human weakness." We do not believe
that Kafka's stories are treatises on religious, metaphysical, or economic problems. Although Kafka has been
lauded for his remarkable descriptions of bureaucracies
and for his prophetic visions of totalitarian states, it is a
fact that he was never seriously committed to the solution of social problems. Only in his early youth did he
join a political organization and only once in his works
does he suggest a measure for the solution of the ills of
society: a monastic order, for bachelors only, based on
vows of poverty (B, 84–85). The people and landscapes
Kafka describes may seem real, but their reality is the
reality of a dream. He had no qualms about writing
about America, a country he had never seen, nor had he
any compunction about depriving the Statue of Liberty
of her torch and replacing it with a sword. This could
not have been an error; some proof reader must have
called it to Kafka's attention, but even if Kafka had been
made aware of the error, he let it stand. Kafka was un-
concerned about distorting reality; he molded it to fit
his inner needs.

Kafka was the most egocentric of all writers. He freely
admitted that his characters were not real people (J, 31);
they were the creations of a dreamer and served only
to illustrate Kafka's needs, problems, and conflicts. We
believe that all of Kafka's heroes are mirror images of
himself, preoccupied obsessively with Kafka's deep inner
problems. Samsa, Raban, K., Joseph K., the hunter

Gracchus, Josephine the singer, the country doctor and his ailing patient, the hunger artist, Kafka's unnamed bachelors, his animal protagonists and hybrids, and his fantasy figures are all self-portraits of Kafka. Many of Kafka's explicators have described the wordplay in which Kafka engaged in identifying his characters with himself. In a diary entry of February 11, 1913, Kafka identified the Bendemann family of "The Judgment" as the Kafkas. For Kafka, Bende (mann), Samsa, and Raban were meaningful anagrams of his name simply because they had the same number of letters, and the configuration of vowels and consonants was similar.

Max Brod pointed out that the name of the engaged bachelor in "Wedding Preparations in the Country," "Raban," was derived from the German word, "rabe" which is a translation of "kavka," the Czech word for "raven." The identity between the hunter Gracchus and Kafka is explained by Wilhelm Emrich who states that "the Latin *Gracchus* is directly related to the word *graculus*," which means jackdaw or raven—a bird with which Kafka identified himself (E, 13). Brod reports that the stationery of Kafka's father's firm was embossed with a beautiful engraving of a raven. Karl is the name of the innocent who is sent away in disgrace to America because he has been seduced by a servant girl and has become the father of her child; Joseph K. is the hero of *The Trial*; *The Castle* was originally written in the first person, later Kafka diminished Joseph K.'s name and named his protagonist "K." The letter "*K*" in these names associates them with Kafka. Josephine, the singer, is the feminine version of Joseph. Heinz Politzer discusses the relationship between Kafka and his numerous bachelors and states that Kafka used these bachelors to express his self-destructive tendencies, observing that by 1913 Kafka's identification with his bachelors had become complete (P, 44). Albérès and de Boisdeffre state unequivocally that Kafka is identified with all of his major characters.

What is so amazing about Kafka's writings is that although almost everyone agrees that he invariably wrote only about himself and depicted his private torments, he has come to be known as the exponent of universal human anguish. Everyone identifies with Kafka's protagonists and translates their fears, problems, and obsessions into his own frame of reference, ignoring Kafka's private inferno. The great genius of Kafka is that he had devised a way of abstracting and distorting his self-images so that they appear as they would in an abstract portrait by Picasso. Kafka painted his various self-images, showing several sides of himself simultaneously, as if from a vantage point beyond space. His mystery, which has resulted in a spate of conflicting interpretations, derives from the fact that his specific images have been abstracted so that they appear to be general and universal. But for Kafka everything he wrote had a unique, personal meaning.

Kafka's images affect his readers as if they were given Kafka's Rorschach protocol and were required to explain Kafka's concepts. Instead of remaining uninvolved and permitting Kafka to define his own images by means of *his* associations with his concepts, they supply Kafka with their own explanations and interpretations. This is not at all remarkable because Kafka's great genius was that he compelled the reader to "project." He himself was amazed at his ability to compel his readers to identify with his characters. He had frequently been puzzled by the inappropriate personal reactions of his audience to his readings. When he read "The Judgment" to his sisters immediately after he had completed it, one of them remarked that the description of the house was like their house. Kafka was astonished and explained that it could not be the Kafka residence because the father would then be living in the bathroom. About a year later, one of his sisters was present when he read the story at Felix Weltsch's house. After he finished the story, Felix Weltsch's father left the room for several moments; then he returned and pointing to the chair he had vacated, he said, "I see this father before me." Again Kafka's sister stated that the house was very much like theirs and again Kafka protested. Kafka had been describing his inner image of his father, who was probably the very antithesis of old Mr. Weltsch in character, and the house he depicted could have borne no resemblance to any house in which the Kafkas had lived. Certainly his sister should have known that her parents would never have chosen the smallest, darkest, dingiest room in the house for their bedroom.

One of Kafka's aphorisms reads: "Confession and the lie are one and the same. In order to be able to confess, one tells lies. One cannot express what one is, for that *is* precisely what one is; one can communicate only what one is not, that is, the lie. Only in the chorus there may be a certain truth" (DF, 308). Does this mean that if Kafka were making a confession in his creative works—he was patently making a confession in his early meditations on his bachelor image—the confession would appear as a lie, which could not be detected except in the "chorus" of all of his writings? Kafka was quixotically honest, but he was also the epitome of ambivalence. He drew a sketch on the margin of one of his letters to Milena in which he depicted himself being torn apart on a rack. If, in his tormented ambivalence, Kafka wanted to reveal his secret as much as he wanted to conceal it, he could not tell a single factual lie. He would therefore be constrained to withhold the key fact, which he obviously did in almost all of his narratives, or to make his confession so ambiguous, so clouded with smoke screens, so evasive, that the secret he was confessing would remain concealed.

We suggest that this was just what Kafka was doing in all of his narratives. We believe that all of Kafka's characters constitute a gallery of self-portraits, painted in the style of Picasso's *Seated Woman*, so that no one could possibly recognize the sitter. We believe that Kafka did this deliberately in order to give "personal proof" of his "human weakness" (a masterpiece of understatement) which he did not dare to reveal. In our analysis of the chorus of Kafka's works, we discovered that Kafka had developed a variety of techniques of obfuscation the most obvious of which was his reluctance to give a credible explanation for the plight of his protagonists. We noticed that when Kafka did reveal important facts, they were scattered helter-skelter throughout his narratives like pieces of an unarranged jigsaw puzzle; moreover, invariably one of the essential pieces was missing. To understand the story, the interpreter would be required not only to arrange the pieces; he would also find it necessary to deduce logically from the facts presented the vital fact (or facts) which Kafka did not choose to disclose. Only when the missing piece was sketched into the puzzle would the story become comprehensible and the truth emerge.

We also discovered that when Kafka told a direct lie in any of his narratives, he became so disturbed or remorseful that he almost immediately after retracted the lie and told the whole truth. We shall demonstrate this in our analysis of his stories. We learned that Kafka's heroes are always at variance with the legal statutes and the religious or ethical standards of their culture. None of Kafka's heroes has done anything wrong; all of them consider themselves innocent. Yet they are treated by their contemporaries as if they were pariahs, criminals, or inhuman. The young boy, whose catastrophic experience we shall discuss in this chapter, admits that he has committed a fault. Since we know that Kafka is always telling the truth, we must believe that he commited a fault, not a crime. However this fault is considered a crime in the eyes of his culture because the bachelor in this story stands outside the law. We discovered that when any of Kafka's protagonists says or thinks he is innocent, he *is* innocent; the fact that he is "outside our people, outside our humanity," and "outside the law" is equally true.

Although Kafka always told the truth, it was seldom the whole truth. He always withheld at least one key fact in order to guard his secret. When he actually told the whole truth, he did it by means of symbolic language so that no one could possibly understand exactly what he was saying. In those stories in which he told the truth, he embellished his revelation with irrelevant, extraneous literary doodles until it was as undecipherable as the script written for the Designer of the torture machine in the penal colony: it was extremely "artistic" but completely incomprehensible.

He skillfully interchanged literal and figurative meanings in order to create confusion. He used irony which was virtually undetectable, therefore he seemed to be telling the truth when he was telling the opposite of the truth. He deliberately used misleading analogies, similes, and metaphors and baffled his readers by his use of understatement and hyperbole. He made blanket generalizations on the basis of a single particular. He presented rationalizations which were indeed true, but they were only a small part of the truth.

He used puns, double entendres, and interchanged the meanings of such words as "schuld," which is the German word for either "debt" or "guilt," so that the reader could not be sure whether he was writing about debts or guilt. He created a secret code in which he substituted his intensely personalized meanings of such ordinary words as music, food, the wound, and fasting. We shall discuss this code at length in the next chapter. He gave innumerable clues as to the explicit meanings of these code words, but none of his interpreters recognized his simple clues. For example, in "The Hunger Artist," the clue lies in the fact that the wild, vigorous, beautiful panther liked the food that was brought to him (PC, 255), which was obviously animal food. The hunger artist fasted because there was no human food that he could swallow. He, like Gregor Samsa of "The Metamorphosis," needed "animal" food. Kafka believed that he made his stories almost transparent. He told Janouch that he did not "introduce miracles into ordinary events." For him the ordinary was a miracle which he simply recorded. He said that he flooded his narratives with dazzling light, "Therefore men close their eyes, and see so little" (J, 74).

There is a fragment of a short story written in the

early pages of Kafka's first diary which is repeated over and over again as if Kafka were experimenting with different versions. Although this sketch is extremely incoherent, we believe it is the most self-revelatory story Kafka ever wrote because it is not written in the language of dreams; moreover the undisclosed fact is almost obvious. Heinz Politzer, whom we consider the most objective and perspicacious of Kafka's explicators, states that in this diary entry Kafka finds the model for all of his major themes and his human and animal protagonists, describing the bachelor as follows:

> "[He] stands once and for all outside our people, outside our humanity," like Josephine the Singer. "He is continually starved" (DI, 26), a description which anticipates the figure of the Hunger Artist. "He can live only as a hermit or a parasite. He is a hermit only by compulsion, once this compulsion is overcome by forces unknown to him, immediately he is a parasite who behaves insolently whenever he possibly can" (DI, 28). This foreshadows the metamorphosis of Gregor Samsa who was changed from a recluse to a parasitic insect. The bachelor has less hold on life "than the trapeze artist in a variety show, who still has a net hung for him below." Such a net will be conspicuously absent during the trapeze act in "First Sorrow." Finally in the moment the writer decides to side with the bachelor, he is heard to cry, "We are outside the law, no one knows it and yet everyone treats us accordingly" (DI, 27), an expression of an idea so basic to Kafka that it anticipates the principal figures of *The Trial* and *The Castle* and their predicament. These figures are united in their common origin in Kafka's diary entry of 1910; they all stand for the bachelor and the bachelor will represent them all. (P, 45)

We believe that in this fragment which Kafka wrote in the secrecy of his first diary, Kafka for the first time incorporated all of the themes and reflections which had always obsessed him, and using literal language rather than the language of dreams, for the first and last time gave the specific reason for his own torment which was later reflected in the anguish of all of his major characters.

The story is indeed disorganized and incoherent. It is not clear whether it is a dialogue between two bachelors or a monologue. In the beginning, two bachelors, who have met several hours earlier are conversing, and there is an attempt to differentiate between them. One of the bachelors has not yet decided to relinquish all social activities and is eager to attend a party to which he had been invited (DI, 29); the older bachelor has become so nihilistic that it makes no difference to him whether he laps up rain water in the gutter or drinks champagne at the elaborate party going on upstairs. The characters soon become so confused that the younger bachelor appears to be telling the older bachelor's story. The quotation marks which had been used to differentiate the two men disappear, and it becomes evident that Kafka is playing a dual role in this story. He is the older, nihilistic bachelor who deplores his miserable, alienated bachelor existence; he is simultaneously a bachelor of Kafka's age (Kafka was twenty-seven years old at that time), who still attends parties in order to attain something that he "lacks" (DI, 24). The portrait of the older bachelor may well be Kafka's projection of the image he thinks he will present when he reaches the age of forty.

The narrator of this fragment describes a catastrophic experience which happened in his youth which impaled him upon a memory of an "everlasting moment of torment." Speaking of himself in the third person, he tells the following story:

"He went astray at that time—which no one can know today, for nothing can be so annihilated as that time —he went astray at that time when he felt his depth lastingly, the way one suddenly notices an ulcer on one's body that until this moment was the least thing on one's body—yes, not even the least, for it appeared not yet to exist and now is more than everything else that we had bodily owned since our birth. If until now our whole person had been oriented upon the work of our hands, upon that which was seen by our eyes, heard by our ears, upon the steps made by our feet, now we suddenly turn ourselves entirely in the opposite direction, like a weather vane in the mountains.

"Now, instead of having run away at that moment, even in this latter direction, for only running away could have kept him on the tips of his toes and only the tips of his toes could have kept him on the earth, instead of that he lay down, as children now and then lie down in the snow in winter in order to freeze to death. He and these children, they know of course that it is their fault for having lain down or yielded in some other way, they know that they should not have done it at any cost, but they cannot know that after the transformation that is taking place in them on the fields or in the cities they will forget every former fault and every compulsion and that they will move about in the new element as if it were their first. But forgetting is not the right word here. The memory of this man has suffered as little as his imagination. But they just cannot move mountains; the man stands once and for all outside our people, outside our humanity, he is continually starved, he has only the moment, the everlasting moment of torment which is followed by no glimpse of a moment of recovery, he has only one thing always: his pain; in all the circumference of the world no second thing that could serve as a medicine." (DI, 25–26)

Already, what protected me seemed to dissolve here in the city. I was beautiful in the early days, for this dissolution takes place as an apotheosis, in which every-thing that holds us to life flies away, but even in flying away illumines us for the last time with its human

light. So I stand before my bachelor and most probably he loves me for it, but without himself really
knowing why." (DI, 28)

The reader should not be disturbed if he finds it difficult to arrive at the meaning of this excerpt. To the best
of our knowledge, Heinz Politzer is the only interpreter
who has made an attempt to unravel this incoherent
fragment. We suggest the the narrator is telling the story
of his homosexual awakening which occurred in his
early youth. In order to indicate how we arrived at this
conclusion, we shall analyze every word of this confession, interpreting it deductively whenever necessary and
interpolating our deductions.

In the first paragraph, the narrator, whom we had
identified with Kafka, states that he went astray when
he discovered some defect within his "depth," or the
core of his personality. He had been unaware of this inner
imperfection until the moment when he went astray. It
was like an "ulcer" or boil, which lies dormant under the
skin and seems nonexistent until it erupts on the skin
and becomes visible. Until then it is the least thing that
could cause concern. Now this defect, which had been
lying invisible in his depth, has become more important
to him than anything he had "bodily owned" since his
birth. It appears that this defect involves his body as well
as his personality. This is confirmed in the next sentence
in which he discusses his "whole person" and his orientation in life in relation to the invisible defect he had discovered in his "depth."

Up to the time the boy discovered the flaw at the root
of his personality, there had been nothing singular about
his orientation in life—it had been indistinguishable
from that of all other boys. Like all other boys, his
"whole person" had been oriented by the work he was
doing ("the work of our hands"), by all of his reactions
to all of the stimuli in his environment ("that which
was seen by our eyes and heard by our ears"), by the
plans he had been making for the future, and the direc-

tion he had been following to achieve his goals (" the steps made by our feet"). His "whole person," by definition, involved his body, his mind, all of his senses, his emotions, and his sexual identification, which is the basic element of one's whole person and one's orientation in life.

When the boy became aware of his inner imperfection, he suddenly turned himself around in an entirely opposite position from the position he had been facing since his birth in common with all other boys. He realized he could no longer see, hear, think, feel, or plan like ordinary boys. Since his sexual orientation was involved in this about-face in orientation, his sexual aims and goals were reversed and had become the opposite of other males. Therefore, instead of reacting in an ordinary way to sexual objects in his environment, he responded in an entirely opposite fashion: whereas other males sought females in their quest for sexual satisfaction, he could achieve sexual gratification only with males. When the boy made this discovery, he precipitously turned himself about in an entirely opposite direction from that which he had been facing at birth, "like a weather vane in the mountains." He had come to the catastrophic realization that he was a homosexual and that he must henceforth face life from the viewpoint of a homosexual in his culture: a viewpoint diametrically opposed to that of other men.

Up to the moment when the boy discovered the inversion of his sexual orientation, he had not given the matter of his orientation a moment's thought. His homosexual orientation had lain latent within his unconscious like an invisible boil until the very moment when it erupted into his consciousness. It had seemed "not yet to exist," it was the "least thing" that concerned him. Now his homosexual orientation is the most important thing that has happened to him since his birth. The sexual identity he had "bodily owned" at birth is no longer his present identity. He knew that his identity as a homosexual would remain with him "lastingly." He "went astray" at that time.

We believe we have explained the first paragraph of the bachelor's confession except for the clauses: "which no one can know today, for nothing can be so annihilated as that time—." The bachelor seems to be saying that his homosexuality is a secret which he has never revealed. He can safely make this confession to his companion because, as we mentioned previously, both bachelors are mirror reflections of Kafka. It is also obvious that Kafka is saying that he has annihilated that time. We know that he has not annihilated his memory of that time because he says that his memory is intact, it "has suffered as little as his imagination." He must therefore mean that he has annihilated his homosexual inclinations and has steadfastly refused to accept them. This appears to be confirmed in another passage of this fragment in which the narrator mentions that he is now "without a center." He also states that when he loses something, he "seeks to get it back by force, though it be transformed, weakened, yes, even though it be his former property only in seeming (which it is for the most part)" (DI, 24). We suggest that this means that he is trying to regain his center of gravity and his heterosexual orientation. He goes to parties, seeking everything "that I lack, the organization of my strength, above all" (DI, 24). He probably hopes that a miracle will occur and that he will regain his equilibrium by falling in love with a woman.

In the second paragraph of this fragment, the narrator tells us that if the boy had run away at the moment when he discovered his homosexual orientation, in any direction whatever, he would have survived and remained on earth. Since he did not run away, he is figuratively no longer on earth: he is dead while he is still alive. Instead of running away, he committed an act tantamount to suicide—as self-immolating an act as lying down in the snow in order to freeze to death. He knew, as did all other children, that if they lie down on the fields or in the cities or yield in some other way, it is their fault. He knew, as did all other children, that he should not do this at any cost. However, he, in common with other children, had no conception of the dire consequences of committing such a fault. They did not know that if they lie down or yield in some other way, a transformation immediately takes place in them on the fields or in the cities. They did not know that after this terrible transformation takes place, they will forget every former fault and every former compulsion. They will be jolted out of the world of other men and will henceforth move about in a "new element" as if they had been born in it. The bachelor can no more forget the moment when he went astray than he can move mountains. He is obsessed with the memory of this catastrophic experience; no medicine on earth can cure his pain. He now stands, "once and for all outside our people, outside our humanity."

In the last episode of the bachelor's confession, he says that he had been protected by his unconsciousness of his homosexual orientation until he came to the city where the dissolution of his innocence and of his life took place. While his life was falling into ruin and his world was dissolving, he experienced an apotheosis. Even though everything that had held him to life flew away at that moment, he was illumined by the human light shed upon his by his apotheosis, which he experienced for the last time. (The bachelor is telling a falsehood; he will retract it later.) The boy was beautiful when he experienced his apotheosis and remains beautiful, for he is still transfigured by the human light which illumined him. His companion loves him for it, but without really knowing why. It appears that his everlasting torment stems from the fact that he must forever renounce the ecstasy he had felt.

This seems to be confirmed in the introduction to this confession in which the bachelor says: "But it is just I who feel my depth much too often and much too strongly to be able to be even only halfway satisfied. And this depth I need but feel uninterruptedly for a quarter of an hour and the poisonous world flows into my mouth like water into that of a drowning man" (DI, 25). The bachelor is saying that he feels his homosexual drives, which emanate from his depth, or the root of his personality, much too strongly and too often to be even halfway satisfied (even if he were to surrender to them). But when he contemplates yielding to temptation even for a quarter of an hour, the "poisonous world" reminds him that it can destroy him. He is drowning in the flood of his unfulfilled desires because he knows that if he does not suppress them, he faces social annihilation.

We mentioned that the bachelor was not telling the truth when he vowed that his first apotheosis would be his last. The bachelor later retracts this falsehood. He tells his acquaintance, who is one of his ilk (since Kafka is playing both roles), that he does not permit himself anything. He prefers to meet his homosexual acquaintances on the most casual basis, as accidentally as he met this companion in front of a church several hours earlier. He must remain a recluse: "for he can live only as a hermit or a parasite. He is a hermit only by compulsion, once this compulsion is overcome by forces unknown to him, at once he is a parasite who behaves insolently whenever he possibly can" (DI, 28). It seems clear that the bachelor is confessing that he yields to temptation when he is overcome by forces beyond his control. At such times he describes himself as a drowned man, who is buoyed up by a current and collides with a swimmer. The corpse can pull the swimmer down with him; nothing at all can save the corpse.

An avalanche of woes descended upon the bachelor after he went astray. He lost his center of gravity when he lost his heterosexual orientation, and is now without a center, a love, a family of his own, and without a profession (DI, 24). (Again he is telling an untruth, but he will atone for it later.) He is continually starved for sexual gratification because the food which nourishes other men has become poison for him. He dare not try to obtain the nourishment he needs for fear of social disaster. He has become "unknowable" and must remain "completely concealed." He is concealed by his profession (which he formerly said he did not have) and by his literary inclinations. (Here he recants his lie by mentioning that he has a profession; then to atone for his falsehood, he gratuitously reveals his identity by mentioning his literary inclinations.)

His nature has become suicidal, "therefore it has teeth only for his own flesh and flesh only for his own teeth" (DI, 24). Since he can find no nourishment in life, he is eating himself up alive. He is outside the law and is forced to conceal himself within an ever-diminishing circle, of which he says:

> "Well this circle indeed belongs to us, but belongs to us only so long as we keep to it, if we move to the side just once, in any chance forgetting of self, in some distraction, some fright, some astonishment, some fatigue, we have already lost it into space, until now we had our noses stuck into the tide of the times, now we step back . . . and are lost. We are outside the law, no one knows it and yet everyone treats us accordingly." (DI, 27)

The bachelor is saying that he must guard himself vigilantly every moment, for if he forgets himself, he is lost. Since he is now facing life from an opposite viewpoint from that of other men, his nose is no longer "stuck into the tide" of his times. For him there is no future: he has only a past which he must annihilate if he wishes to remain within the law. As a homosexual, he is "outside the law, no one knows it and yet everyone treats" him accordingly.

The inquisitive reader will notice that Kafka resolutely adhered to his practice of withholding one key fact in this story, which we shall entitle "Moment of Torment" for practical purposes. Kafka did not choose to mention that the boy was not alone. It is obvious that we must insert this missing fact into the story. The boy could not have been alone because he could not have become aware of his homosexual orientation in a vacuum. Some male had to be with this boy to spark his sudden consciousness of his homosexual orientation, of which he had been totally unaware until the moment when he went astray. Kafka tells us that the boy was the victim, not the aggressor: his only fault was that he lay down or yielded and did not run away. He must have been in the presence of some male who made homosexual overtures and suddenly became aware of his overpowering desire to yield even though he knew it was suicidal. Instead of running away, he lay down somewhere in the city or yielded in some way. He could not have known at that time that once he had been illumined by the light of his apotheosis, he would forever after be lured by an overwhelming desire to repeat his ecstatic experience.

In Politzer's interpretation of this diary entry, he discusses Kafka's obsession with dirt and filth and his reaction formation against them which was evidenced in his excessive concern with the cleanliness of his heroes' surroundings. Politzer observes: "The fascination with dirt and obscenity may very well have been the enigmatic depth" which the bachelor "claimed to have discovered in the core of his personality" (P, 43). Politzer then explains: "This depth which threatened to engulf him [Kafka] and barred him from normal intercourse was necessary to complete the image, he [Kafka] formed of himself as a bachelor. Surrendering to it, plunging into it even 'for a quarter of an hour,' showed him the unsaintliness of his being. . . . It was this depth that lured, drew and drove him toward the dirt the very thought of which filled him with horror" (P, 43). Politzer then says: "The key word is 'depth' which compares to a boil and . . . which points to an abode of filth and obscenity in his own soul. When he discovered this 'depth' in the recesses of sex, the bachelor 'went astray.' Since then he has been engaged in a ceaseless escape from an equally unending temptation" (P, 44). Politzer, who identified both bachelors with Kafka, was cognizant of the great significance of the moment when the boy went astray because he remarks that young Kafka became a "prospective bachelor" at that time. He seems unaware, however, that the temptation which the boy resolved to renounce was for him an apotheosis which transfigured him and made him feel God-like. There is nothing in this specific passage or within the entire fragment to indicate that the bachelor considers his "depth," which we defined as the seat of his homosexual orientation, to be filthy or obscene. We concede, however that Kafka indicated within the totality of his writings that he was extremely ambivalent about his homosexual orientation. In "The Country Doctor," he regards it as a pigsty which provides him with unearthly horses which transport him figuratively; however his homosexual inclinations also banish him to an icy realm in which he must live in uncompromising loneliness.

It would be the height of futility to attempt to uncover concrete evidence to substantiate our interpretation of this story. There is a superfluity of textual evidence, but it lies buried under Kafka's remarkable techniques of obfuscation. Nowhere in the chorus of his works does Kafka admit openly that he is a homosexual. All such admissions are completely concealed in symbolic language or by means of Kafka's numerous smoke screens which almost obliterate such confessions. In our analysis of the chorus of Kafka's creative works, his diaries, notebooks, conversations, and intimate letters, we shall try to dissipate Kafka's smoke screens in order to arrive at his specific meaning, which is the sole purpose of this book.

It is necessary to emphasize that we did not arrive at our thesis that Kafka considered himself to be a homosexual solely on the basis of our interpretation of the story of "Moment of Torment." This incoherent fragment was chosen as our introductory chapter only because it incorporates all of Kafka's themes and philosophical reflections and because it describes most of his major characters. The story of the homosexual awakening is retold with consummate artistry in "Investigations of a Dog" (ch. 3), but it is incomprehensible to the uninitiated reader who is not familiar with Kafka's substitution code which we shall discuss at length in the next chapter. It is only when one reads the totality of Kafka's writings that it becomes apparent that the predicament of all of his heroes is based on the fact that they are all homosexuals. We shall try to demonstrate that if this thesis is accepted, all of Kafka's incomprehensible stories become quite meaningful.

2

The Psyche of a Homosexual

In most critical studies it is both needless and tasteless to discuss such private matters as the sexual orientation of the author, but it is impossible to arrive at the specific meaning of Kafka's creative works unless one has the key to the catastrophe which occurred previously in the life of each of Kafka's major characters which accounts for his arrest, his dehumanization, his rejection from the family circle, his exclusion from all of humanity, his trial, his judgment, his punishment, or his execution. Kafka remains Kafkaesque simply because he chooses to be silent on this extremely crucial matter.

It is for this reason that we must state that an internal examination of all of Kafka's creative works, as well as his diaries, letters, conversations, and dreams, reveals that Kafka considered himself to be a homosexual; and all of his major characters, both human and animal, who are mirror images of Kafka, suffer eternal torment because they are all members of the most despised, the most maligned, and the most harrassed of all minority groups. Whether or not Kafka was in point of fact a homosexual according to modern definitions of homosexuality is irrelevant and immaterial from the viewpoint of this study, the sole purpose of which is to arrive at the meaning of Kafka's incomprehensible narratives. It is not within the province of this book to engage in polemics with psychologists, biologists, and bisexual evangelists of today to determine whether or not Kafka, who was seventeen years old at the turn of the century, and who died in 1924 at the age of forty-one, was correct in his assessment of his psychosexual imbalance. Concepts of homosexuality have changed radically in the past seventy-five years. Today definitions of homosexuality and evaluations of what constitutes "psychological" masculinity or femininity are as varied as the biologists, sociologists, and psychologists who define these concepts.

Abram Kardiner, one of Kafka's contemporaries, who worked with Freud in the 1920s, published a book in 1954 entitled *Sex and Morality* in which he said: "Fifty years ago there was no question about what a homosexual was, a person who was sexually aroused by, and anticipated and consummated orgiastic experience with, a male of the same sex" (SAM, 163). He also pointed out that there are "true homosexuals who have never had a single contact with a male in their entire lives, being too fearful of the consequences" (SAM, 186). Kardiner described Kafka's predicament cogently and accurately. We shall demonstrate that Kafka revealed behind his smoke screens within the chorus of his works, and openly within his diary, that he was sexually aroused by other men (ch. 6); throughout his life he "fasted," because he was terrified of the consequences.

We shall analyze the blurred textual evidence gleaned from the totality of Kafka's creative works, dreams, conversations, letters, and diaries to prove that Kafka envisioned himself as a man with a woman's "nature" (PC, 43). In symbolic language he made it clear that he considered his homosexual orientation the best part of himself and the "indestructible element" in himself. He described himself as a man afflicted with an "invisible wound," "an inner imperfection" which manifested itself by making him a female with a male outer body. We shall analyze this concept later in this chapter.

He had a deep aversion to his hybrid male-female body and systematically tried to destroy it. When he became tubercular in 1917, he realized that he had torn himself "apart like a fish" (DF, 109). He made no seri-

ous effort to cure himself of his disease; rather he greeted
it with open arms because it freed him from the necessity
of violating his nature by getting married. He broke his
second engagement to Felice Bauer and took a rest cure
at Zürau for eight months. In 1920, in a letter to Milena,
he recalled that idyllic period which he considered to be
the best time of his life. He thought that he was facing
death; therefore he had confined himself exclusively to
that which he believed was "unquestionable" within
himself. He felt free of his obsession to get married because he was protected by the "shelter" of his illness.
He felt that he "didn't have to change much" of himself; he had only to "retrace more firmly, the narrow out-
lines of" his "nature" (M, 68).

Kafka's happiness at Zürau was of a brief duration. In
1919, he became engaged to Julie Wohryzec, the girl
mentioned in his letter to his father. He was still engaged
to Julie, with no intention whatever of marrying her although they had already looked for an apartment, when
he met Milena Jesenská in 1920 and fell in love for the
first time—as deeply as he could fall in love with a
woman. At the climax of his ardent courtship, he wrote
Milena, who was the translator of his works into Czech:
"And perhaps it isn't you I really love, but the existence
presented to me by you" (M, 96). Milena represented
Kafka's last hope of salvation. She was a pillar of fire
that would lead him through the wilderness in which he
had been wandering for thirty-eight years and bring him
to the promised land of normalcy. She was a savior who
would intercede for him in heaven (M, 83), and save
him from drowning in the sea of his aberrant sexuality.

Kafka also welcomed his "amiable disease" (tuberculosis), because it made it possible for him to return as a
sick child to the home of his father, to whom he was
attached as if by an umbilical cord, and whom he loved,
hated, admired, and scorned above everyone else on
earth (ch. 4). In his famous letter to his father, Kafka
openly accused his father of having "blocked" the road
to his development (DR, 143). As a result, "The boy

who was about to take his first leap into life got stuck halfway" (DF, 187). Kafka could not tell his father that because the road to his development had been blocked, he had taken a deviant path; but he hinted darkly that a fatal wound had been inflicted upon him. He told his father that they were so different and so dangerous to each other in their difference, that "if anyone had tried to calculate in advance, how I, the slowly developing child, and you, the full-grown man, would stand to each other, he would have assumed that you would simply trample me underfoot so that nothing was left of me. Well, that didn't happen. Nothing alive can be calculated. But perhaps something worse happened" (DF, 141).

Something infinitely worse had happened. Instead of taking a leap into life, we believe that Kafka had taken a leap into limbo and for the rest of his life, like "The Hunter Gracchus," he was dead within his lifetime (DII, 196). His ship had lost its rudder and he could no longer direct it the way he wanted it to go (M, 202). Moreover, he did not even know which way he wanted to direct it. He became an outlaw in the eyes of his culture and lost his citizenship in the world of ordinary men. He wrote in his diary: "I am now a citizen of this other world, whose relationship to the ordinary one is the relationship of the wilderness to cultivated land. (I have been forty years wandering from Canaan)" (DII, 213). Because of the wound inflicted upon him by his father, he had been condemned to wander in the wilderness, doomed never to reach the promised land.

Kafka conceded in his letter to his father that even with the mildest and most indulgent of fathers, he might have become "a shy, nervous person, but it is a long dark road from there to where I have really come to" (DF, 170). Our thesis is that the long dark road Kafka had arrived at led in an opposite direction from the road travelled by other men. Despite his fierce yearning for a wife and children of his own (DII, 207), Kafka could not follow the road which led to the normal gratifications of life. His world had turned topsy-turvy and he was facing in an opposite direction from that which he had faced at birth. He explained to Milena that when "the Earth turns to the right . . . I would have to turn to the left to make up for the past" (M, 219).

Kafka had barred no holds in his scathing denunciation of his father's pedagogy. He described the abuse, threats, malicious scorn, and spiteful laughter which had characterized his father's method of bringing up his children and of dealing with his relatives and employees; but when the time came to tell his father why marriage was barred for him, his letter to his father became as opaque and Kafkaesque as his literary creations—and for the same reason: *Kafka chose to remain silent on the crucial issue.* He wrote: "I shall have to be silent on certain matters that it is still too hard for me to confess —to you and to myself. I say this in order that, if the picture as a whole should be somewhat blurred here and there, you should not believe that what is to blame is any lack of evidence; on the contrary, there is evidence that might make the picture unbearably stark" (DF, 170). He told his father: "My writing was all about you; all I did there, after all, was to bemoan what I could not bemoan upon your breast" (DF, 177).

We suggest that the "unbearably stark" evidence that Kafka could not disclose to his father became the subject matter of all of his creative works. Kafka bemoaned in his literary creations the fact that because his father had blocked the path to his development, he had taken a deviant path. It is our thesis that the totality of Kafka's works constitute an autobiographical confession written in symbolic form and with the use of a secret code because Kafka did not dare to reveal that he considered himself a sexual deviant. Torn apart by his passion to tell the truth and reveal his true image and his fear of removing his mask and inviting social disaster, Kafka painted a gallery of unrecognizable self-portraits, depicting his true self and describing the insoluble dilemma confronting him as a sexual deviant in his culture. Obviously Kafka depicted his self-portraits as he envisioned himself. It becomes self-evident that we must view them as he painted them if we are to arrive at his meaning.

It is our conviction that "Moment of Torment," which we believe describes Kafka's homosexual seduction, is not only the source of all of his themes and images; it also provides the only credible explanation for the catastrophe which descended upon all of Kafka's heroes which catapulted them out of the normal world of ordinary men and made them pariahs in the eyes of their fellowmen. Wilhelm Emrich, who made a monumental study of Kafka's themes and imagery, confirms our thesis that Kafka's heroes take a leap out of the normal conceptual world of ordinary men (E, 12). Emrich, who does not identify the cataclysm which jolted Kafka and his heroes out of the ordinary, commonplace world, maintains that this phenomenon was the "source not only of their sufferings and despair, but also of all their 'battles,' of their most demanding objectives, of their clairvoyant perceptions; indeed, even of their almost hubristic hopes of creating an indestructible world" (E, 12).

We differ with Emrich on only one point—Kafka's heroes do not strive to create an "indestructible world." They are concerned only with what they consider to be the indestructible element within themselves—their deviant sexual orientation. Their most hubristic hope is to be permitted to live in this world in their true image and to be treated as human beings. For Kafka and his heroes, our absurd world is Paradise. Other men have eaten of the tree of knowledge, yet they remain in Paradise because they can nourish themselves on the tree of life. Kafka and his heroes have also eaten of the tree of knowledge, but the fruit of the tree of life is denied them (DF, 43). They can find no nourishment in this world and must therefore starve (E, 55; DF, 41; ch. 5).

In discussing "K." of *The Castle*, Emrich observes: "Metaphorically, K., like Samsa, has turned into an animal that has fallen out of the [normal] categories of existence and is now seeking 'nourishment.' In contrast with everyone else, his 'self' no longer fits into purported existence, but is a hungry extrahuman being" (E, 484). We revert to our thesis: Kafka's heroes are always hungry because the nourishment they need (deviant sexual gratification) is unattainable for them in their culture. The very fact that they yearn for this unattainable nourishment makes them incomprehensible to all other men who regard them as inhuman, animals, and outlaws.

Perhaps in compensation for the fact that he was forced to live a lie, Kafka became quixotically obsessed with the need to tell the whole truth. He did not feel responsible for his aberrant sexuality (DI, 19), and therefore he did not feel unduly guilty. He reproached his father, his mother, and an entire retinue of authority figures for having emasculated him and transformed him into a female with a male outer body. In righteous indignation, he claimed from the "corrupters" of his youth, who came to represent for him all the authority figures in the universe, his right to exist in the image they had created, exclaiming: "I demand from their hands the person I now am" (DI, 18).

He refused to be deceived by all the words of all authority figures everywhere and questioned every law and every tradition because the obsolete, inhuman, and illogical laws of his culture condemned him to a living death. His writings were a protest against all human authority figures as well as an act of defiance against an authoritarian God, whom he identified with his father, and in whom he had very little faith. As early as 1904, he wrote his "mysterious" (M, 116) first friend, Oskar Pollak: "God does not want me to write; but I, I must" (E, 65). His creative works were a "reward for service to the Devil" (E, 65), a "leap out of murderer's row" (DII, 212), but they were simultaneously "a struggle for self-preservation" (DII, 75). Although he had enormous literary talents which clamored for expression, Kafka's motive for writing was different from that of all other authors. He wrote primarily for the purpose of setting "his extremely complex soul in order" (B, 17). He probed endlessly into himself, conducting what was in essence a self-analysis, but which he always refused to call a self-analysis, in order to cure himself of his affliction or to gain the strength to bear it. Long before Sigmund Freud began to question the curative aspects of psychoanalysis, Kafka came to the conclusion that the "therapeutic part of psychoanalysis" was a "hopeless error" (M, 217). Nevertheless he persisted in his self-probings, reporting his psychosexual maturation on his deathbed in his story of "Josephine the Singer, or the Mouse Folk."

He painted his self-portraits "with greatest complete-ness, with all the incidental consequences, as well as with entire truthfulness" (DI, 42), and was terrified that the portraits he depicted might be recognized: "What a chill pursued me all day out of what I had written! How great the danger was" (DI, 43). Kafka was no shop-keeper concerned about the sale of his wares. He was completely self-obsessed and wrote only about himself and for himself (J, 26; M, 131), painting a gallery of self-portraits depicting his problem and writing on only one theme—the plight of a sexual deviant in his culture. Tongue in cheek, he portrayed himself in his description of Titorelli, the Court painter of *The Trial*, who emu-lated Kafka's unique, repetitive performance, painting innumerable identical portraits of all of the Judges and countless identical landscapes.

Kafka worked assiduously to create devices of mystifi-cation and a secret code which no one would be able to decipher so that he could tell the whole truth without fear of harrassment. His narrating dog remarks: "The essence of a secret code is that it remain a mystery." Kafka's code has remained a mystery because his expli-cators saw fit to provide Kafka with their own explana-tions of Kafka's enigmatic concepts instead of searching for all of Kafka's associations with the themes and images he used, not only within the chorus of his creative works but also in his dreams, intimate letters, and conversations.

To create the key words of his code, Kafka used ordinary, commonplace words, such as: wound, food, music, the road, the way, schnapps, etc.; he divested these words of their ordinary conceptual meanings and substituted his intensely personal meanings which were always related to his problem and his secret. For example, the invisible ulcer, which had erupted into his consciousness at the time of his homosexual seduction, which he described in "Moment of Torment," became one of Kafka's key code images. This "invisible wound" or "inner imperfection" represented Kafka's feeling of bodily disfigurement, associated with his deviant sexual orientation. Since Kafka identified himself with his major human and animal characters, a great many of his protagonists share his disfigurement. The investigating dog sensed "a spot where there was a small crack" (E, 181); he suffered from a "slight maladjustment" which was Kafka's euphemism for his deviant sexuality. (Kafka was a past master of understatement!) Kafka's Ape has a wound on his right hip and another on his cheek, which were inflicted upon him by the cruel, wanton shots of so-called civilized men.

So close was Kafka to his unconscious because of his incessant self-analysis that the same imagery appears in his creative works which occurs in his dreams. In one of his dreams Kafka identifies himself with a disfigured actress by giving her the name of "Frank-el." (Kafka was called "Frank" by some of his friends.) This actress practically usurps Kafka's place by climbing "right over the back of the seat" in the theatre in which Kafka is sitting. She has a "scratched, bloodshot spot, the size of a doorknob" on her right hip (DI, 155), exactly where Kafka's Ape and Mr. Bendemann of "The Judgment," bear their scars. The country doctor's young patient suffers from an identical, lethal wound which is at first imperceptible. Only after the doctor is inspired by his whinnying horses to reexamine his patient, does he discover the open wound which is as big as the palm of his hand, crawling with thick, long, horrible, bloody worms.

Gregor Samsa awakens on the morning of his metamorphosis to find a painful open wound on his belly (PC, 68). The Russian friend in "The Judgment," insists upon remaining a "permanent bachelor" because he, like all of Kafka's bachelors, suffers from a "latent disease" (ch. 4).

All of Kafka's characters who are the possessors of wounds, scars, spots, blemishes, latent diseases, bodily disfigurements, or malformations; or are afflicted with some "slight" or egregious inner imperfection, suffer from the same malady—deviant sexuality. When the wound has healed and a scar has formed, the person or animal appears to be making a good social adjustment, but this adjustment is only superficial. It is like the behavior of the Ape, who sends "A Report to an Academy" describing his remarkable progress in humanization but who commits grave social blunders, pulling down his trousers before his audiences to exhibit his wound. The Ape self-righteously defends this breach of etiquette, exclaiming: "when the plain truth is in question, great minds discard the niceties of refinement" (PC, 175).

Georg's father in "The Judgment," has a unique wound—a battle scar, which we will discuss in our analysis of this story (ch. 4). The bedridden Lawyer Huld in *The Trial*, whose name means "heavenly grace" has assumed the role of a savior and has arrogantly usurped the illnesses of his deviant "upper class" clients in order to lead them to salvation. Lawyer Huld demands complete faith and abject obeisance from the accused, who are always guilty despite the fact that they may not have sinned. He reduces his clients to inhuman beings who grovel at his feet while he overwhelms them with boundless guilt and deep despair.

Homosexuals frequently see diseased and deformed human beings and animals on projective tests of personality such as the Rorschach and the Thematic Apperception Test (TAT). These responses reflect important etiological features in the dynamics of these individuals. In Kafka's case, he associated his wound with his father's consistent rejection of his love and of every aspect of his individuality from early childhood (DF, 138–96). Because of his father's persistent rejection, "Kafka could not establish an identification with his father, therefore he could not become a father" (CHRL, 73).

We mentioned that the theme of bodily disfigurement, which obsessed Kafka in the totality of his writings, also appears in his dreams which are sometimes indistinguishable from his creative works. One theme appears in Kafka's dreams which does not appear in his creative works: the theme of the masculinized woman. Calvin Hall and Richard Lind, who made an objective analysis of the content of Kafka's dreams, observe that Kakfka's "masculinized" woman is a "peculiar," distinctive," and "unusual" feature in men's dreams. These authors report one dream in which a girl is playing the role of a male impersonator on the stage (DI, 142–44; CHRL, 20) and another dream in which a female is dressed in men's clothing (DI, 153–56). They also mention a dream in which Kafka meets Milena in Vienna and notices that they are both wearing outer garments of the same cloth. He comments upon her masculine appearance (M, 61–64). Hall and Lind state that Kafka identifies himself with Milena in this dream as well as in the following extremely significant dream in which Kafka sees himself becoming transformed into a woman:

> Last night I dreamt about you. What happened in detail I can hardly remember, all I know is that we kept merging into one another, I was you, you were me. Finally you somehow caught fire. . . . I took an old coat and beat you with it. But again the transmutations began and it went so far that you were no longer even there, instead it was I who was on fire and it was also I who beat the fire with the coat. (M, 207)

Hall and Lind comment: "Although the sexual symbolism in this dream is transparent, it is the transformation of a man into a woman, and a woman into a man that we wish to point out as being of significance. Kafka not only sees women as being masculine, but he also sees himself as changing into a woman, an extremely rare happening in male dreams" (CHRL, 21).

We venture the hypothesis that Kafka, who hinted in his writings that he thought of himself as an actor who was playing the role of a male, identified himself with the male impersonator, the two women in men's clothing, and with the disfigured actress he saw in his dreams. We suggest that the dream in which Kafka became transformed into Milena expressed in dream language Kafka's *conscious* desire to be transformed into a woman. That Kafka was consciously aware of this desire, which filled him with terror, is evidenced in a letter he wrote to Milena in which he confessed that he was drowning in fear because of an inner conspiracy against himself which made him yearn to be a woman. He wrote: "What I'm afraid of, afraid of with wide-open eyes, helplessly drowned in fear . . . is only this inner conspiracy against myself . . . which is perhaps based on the fact that I who, in the great Game of Chess . . . against all the rules of the game and to the confusion of the game, even want to occupy the place of the Queen—" (M, 73; CHRL, 80).

Kafka did not dare to play the role of the "Queen" because of his "fear of people" (M, 221). He had very little faith in man's humanity to man. Rather than face the world in his true image and put mankind to a "truly world-redeeming test" (M, 143), he preferred, like Gregor Samsa, "slowly to creep up the wall" (M, 143; ch. 5). Since he could not violate his nature by playing the role of a man, and dared not play that of a woman, he became a male impersonator. He was a consummate actor with a "pronounced talent for" metamorphosis (DI, 71), and played that role with such impeccable artistry that none of his contemporaries even suspected that he thought of himself as a woman in men's clothing. It is perhaps relevant to point out that homosexuals frequently see women in men's clothing, or men in women's clothing on projective tests such as the Rorschach; they also find it difficult to distinguish the sex of the individuals on the Rorschach and the TAT.

In one of his dreams, Kafka sees a hybrid—half-donkey and half-greyhound that was extremely cautious. It was rumored that this donkey had "always held itself erect like a human being. . . . But actually that was not correct" (DI, 119). Kafka thought of himself as a hybrid and considered himself to be an anomaly of nature so bizarre that he believed he belonged to no known human or animal species. In a diary entry, he asks himself what it is that binds him to human beings rather than to "the penholder in your hand for example? Because you belong to the same species? But you don't belong to the same species, that's the very reason why you raised this question" (DII, 199).

In order to arrive at the meaning of Kafka's concept of "music," (Kafka's code word for either heterosexual or homosexual interactions), we found it necessary to explore all of Kafka's associations with "music" within his dreams, intimate letters, conversations, diaries, and creative works. Kafka had always been deeply distressed by his inability to appreciate music. It became for him a symbol of his incapacity to participate in all of the major gratifications of other men; a constant proof of his distance from other men who responded passionately to the charms of both music and heterosexuality. He told Janouch: "When I think I understand nothing about my great friends' greatest passion, about music, a kind of gentle, bitter-sweet sadness takes hold of me. It is only a breath of wind, an air of death. In a moment, it has gone. Yet it makes me realize how illimitably far away I am even from those who are nearest to me, and so an evil look comes on my face" (J, 136–37).

Since Kafka was completely deaf to the charms of music, he obviously could not have reacted to it either with pleasure or displeasure; it would have been virtually inaudible to him. Yet in another conversation with Janouch, Kafka remarked: "Music creates new, subtler,

more complicated, and therefore more dangerous pleasures" (J, 139–40). Kafka could not have been discussing
"music" in its ordinary conceptual sense. He was enig-
matically referring to his "original" personal concept of
music which he associated with dangerous pleasures of a
new, subtle, and complicated nature. He also associated
"music" with sensuality in this conversation, stating:
"Music is a multiplication of sensuous life." Kafka thus
associated his personal concept of music with his great
friends' greatest passions; with the illimitable distance
between him and his dearest friends; with his alienation
from all of humanity; and with new, dangerous, sensual
pleasures of a subtle, complicated nature.

In a letter to Milena, in which he commended her
for her excellent translation of one of his stories, Kafka
explained: "music is connected with 'fear.' On this oc-
casion the wound broke open for the first time during
one long night" (M, 191). Music was therefore also associated with "fear" in relation to the breaking open of
the wound, which was Kafka's euphemism for his homosexual orientation. Music was also associated with "dirt"
and "Hell" in a letter in which Kafka confessed: "I'm
dirty, Milena, infinitely dirty, which is why I make so
much fuss about purity. No people sing with such pure
voices as those who live in deepest Hell" (M, 185–86).
In one of his extremely enigmatic letters to Milena, Kafka
warned her that "musically judged," any relationship
between them would constitute a superhuman attachment which would result in their mutual immolation.
He wrote: "if therefore—musically judged—you were
willing to renounce the whole world in order to step
down to me, [you] . . . would have to reach *beyond*
yourself in a superhuman way, *beyond* yourself so power-
fully that in doing so you might be torn to shreds, stum-
ble, disappear (and I, no doubt, with you)" (M, 111).

Within his creative writings, in order to distinguish
between homosexuals and heterosexuals, Kafka differentiates the music of ordinary men, to which he and all
of his protagonists are completely deaf, from the music

to which his deviant characters, human and animal, respond with fervor. In "Investigations of a Dog," which we shall discuss at length in the next chapter, this distinction is made crystal clear. The music which had surrounded the young dog since his infancy (heterosexual activity), had made no impression upon him. The music of the performing dogs was quite different—that music was a "sin" and an "abomination" (GW, 15). The innocent narrating dog had found the performance of the musical dogs so peculiar that he could hardly believe that the performing dogs belonged to the dog species. He felt compelled to instruct these sinful dogs in the precepts of morality, but he could not bring himself to condemn them because he had responded so ecstatically to their music.

Kafka differentiates his homosexual characters from ordinary men by describing their reactions to music. All of Kafka's deviant heroes are deaf to the ordinary music of the world. They respond only to a kind of music that is sinful and an abomination. We digress briefly to remind the reader that since Kafka's heroes mirror their author, they share all of his personality traits. They are impatient, suicidal, incomprehensible to their fellowmen, and completely deaf to their music. In "The Departure" (DS, 200) the suicidal bachelor is impatient to escape from a world which offers him nothing but torment. His only goal is "Out of here!" He is so incomprehensible that the servant cannot understand his simple orders. Therefore, when he asks him to saddle his horse, the servant ignores him.

The impatient bachelor must perforce go to the stable to saddle his horse himself. While doing this, he hears the sound of a trumpet and asks the servant the meaning of the trumpet call. The servant, who is heterosexual, "knew nothing and had heard nothing." He is completely deaf to the music of the homosexual bachelor; it is as inaudible to him as is the music of ordinary men to Kafka's heroes. Kafka frequently complained that he suffered from insomnia because he heard the blare of

the "trumpets of the sleepless night" (M, 46). Heterosexuals do not hear these trumpets; therefore they sleep
peacefully. In Kafka's imagery only the guilty are in-
somniacs; the innocent sleep like babes.

Once while discussing a dream in which Milena rejected him, another time when Milena rejected him in
reality, Kafka commented that he found his strength in
being completely unmusical (M, 62, 161). In both cases,
Kafka seems to have been consoling himself by recalling
that he was deaf to Milena's music. He told Milena that
he liked to look into her eyes and hold her hands: "That's
about all" (M, 171). An ambiance of fear pervaded
Kafka's courtship of Milena. He confessed that the fear
emanated from his lack of desire (M, 165).

That Kafka's musicians are not musical in the ordinary sense is made crystal clear in his narratives. None
of them needs musical instruction. In *Amerika*, the
women dressed as angels who sit on high pedestals,
produce a cacophony of excruciating sounds from their
excellent instruments. Karl Rossman, who never played
a trumpet in his life, climbs to the top of one of the
pedestals and plays an "angel's" trumpet with such
artistry that he wins the plaudits of all the angels. Karl
had had only the most rudimentary instruction in music
and could hardly read a note; yet when his American
uncle presented him with a piano, Karl "set great hopes
on his piano playing and sometimes unashamedly
dreamed, at least before falling asleep, of the possibility
that it might exert a direct influence upon his life in
America" (A, 43). This seemingly absurd reverie becomes meaningful only if we realize that Karl is pre-
dominantly homosexually oriented. He hopes to find
freedom in this brave new world to live in his true image
and daydreams of influencing others who share his desires to respond to his music. When Karl plays the piano
for Clara, who is aggressively heterosexual and against
whose physical amatory assaults Karl would have de-
fended himself with a stone chisel if one had been available (A, 86), Clara sits "frozen with embarrassment"

at the quality of his performance (A, 90). Her fiancé, Mack, who is bisexual, reacts enthusiastically. Mack never despised "players of any kind" (A, 91).

Gregor Samsa could not appreciate music while he retained his human form. Only after he had become an animal did he respond to his sister's music (ch. 5). Josephine, the mouse singer, was admittedly an indifferent musician, yet she had no difficulty in attracting a large, appreciative, loyal, youthful audience that admired her posturings even if they did not admire her piping. Josephine was "outside the law." She endangered the community by her music (PC, 270). Carl Woodring identified her as a male impersonator who was a member of a Jewish theatrical group (FKT, 72). Josephine is the feminine version of Joseph K. of *The Trial* and K. of *The Castle*. We shall have more to say about Josephine later.

It becomes obvious when one examines the chorus of Kafka's associations with his concept of music, that Kafka, like Shakespeare, believed that music is the "food of love," but Kafka differentiated between two kinds of music and two kinds of love. Kafka's characters respond to a peculiar kind of piercing, ear-shattering music, a piping, howling, or yodeling, or army songs which lonely soldiers sing to each other in their barracks at night. Music is associated with piercing pain as well as with ecstasy. The performers are much more important than the performance and their bodily movements, representing homosexual posturings, are infinitely more important than their musical ability. "Silence" is an important aspect of music. Kafka's musical performers are obligated to keep the "silence" (GW, 37). They can never discuss their musical experiences even with their dearest friends. Most of Kafka's characters who sing or play an instrument are either deviant personalities or the love objects of deviant personalities. They are never true musicians. Rank amateurs with no musical training, knowledge, or ability are able to delight their audiences if their listeners are attuned to their particular kind of music—homosexuality or deviant sexuality.

That food and music are very closely interrelated concepts is indicated by the fact that the future researches of the investigating dog are to be made on the border region between the "two sciences" of "food" and "music." Food is differentiated from music qualitatively; it represents the simple appeasement of deviant appetites. Kafka and his heroes have no appetite for the food of ordinary men—heterosexuality. They need the food of animals. Nor can Kafka's unevolved human beings or bachelors relish alcoholic beverages. Most of his homosexual characters find beer and harsh alcoholic beverages very distasteful.

Kafka had always associated drinking alcoholic beverages with masculinity. In his letter to his father, he stated that his father had shown him love and approval only when he acted in what his father considered to be a manly fashion—when he stood up erect and saluted briskly like a soldier, when he drank beer with his meals, or when he imitated other "virile" attributes of his father. Kafka deeply resented the fact that his father never accepted him as an individual and reacted by loathing everything that his father liked. Throughout his life alcoholic beverages nauseated him. In his code, Kafka equated the drinking of alcoholic beverages with heterosexuality. Just as his inability to appreciate music reminded him of the illimitable distance between himself and all of humanity, his loathing for alcoholic beverages must have made him profoundly aware of his incapacity to participate in the simple gratifications of ordinary men.

Since Kafka like Freud believed that homosexuality is a symptom of arrested psychosexual development, he concluded that in order to develop psychosexually, he must evolve from his "animal" state to attain the status of a man. In "A Report to an Academy," Kafka portrays himself as the Ape and describes his remarkable progress in evolution. He had forced himself to travel at a meteoric pace through aeons of evolutionary progress in the span of five years and had learned how to "ape" the cultured, modern European of his time. He had tortured himself and been tortured by his instructors, who held burning cigarettes against his flesh so that he could master the theory and practice of the "ritual" of drinking schnapps, which was Kafka's image for heterosexual interactions.

Like the Ape who thought with his belly, Kafka felt intuitively that if he could convince himself and others that he could perform like a man, he might lose his ape-like nature and thereby become "comprehensible" to other men. In this story, the Ape is able to speak for the first time after he demonstrates that he can swallow a bottle of schnapps. For the first time he becomes comprehensible to his fellowmen who welcome him into the human fraternity. However, the Ape had not truly become humanized despite his demonstration of his ability to drink schnapps. His aversion to alcohol returned immediately after his demonstration. Although he occasionally drinks schnapps to preserve his human status, he is still unable to mate with a human female. His bewildered spouse is a chimpanzee.

Since Kafka's writings are autobiographical, it is not at all surprising that he was never able to tolerate alcohol until the last year of his life when he achieved a psychosexual balance. In the summer of 1923, Kafka fell in love with Dora Dymant, a Polish orthodox Jewess, who was about half his age. Shortly before he met Dora, Kafka had confessed to Milena that unlike his hero, Alexander the Great, he had been unable to cut the "Gordian knot" which linked him with his father (M, 216; PC, 135). When Kafka met Dora, he cut the cord which had attached him to his father and left Prague to live with Dora in Berlin. He reported his psychosexual maturation in "Josephine the Singer, or the Mouse Folk."

Kafka insisted upon appending a subtitle to this narrative although there is no mention of mice anywhere in this story. Unable to speak because he was suffering from tuberculosis of the larynx, Kafka wrote Brod a note, saying: "Subtitles like this are not very pretty, but in this case it has perhaps a special meaning. The title has something of a balance." We believe that Kafka was referring obliquely to the psychosexual balance he had achieved which made it possible for him to live comfortably with Dora. The story is a eulogy on the disappearance of Josephine, the singer, who had permanently withdrawn from the community because her audiences refused to concede to her inflexible demand that she be exempted from working at her exhausting daily job so that she could concentrate upon developing her art. Moreover she had insisted upon total unqualified appreciation and recognition of her art, which she complained no one any longer understood. Kafka, who was at that time seriously ill, was no longer "carried away" by music. "Tranquil peace" was the music he loved best. Although Kafka was in the terminal stage of tuberculosis when he met Dora, for the first time in his life he was truly happy. For the first time he desperately wanted to live and followed his doctor's orders "with exactitude" and without protest. He suddenly lost his loathing for alcoholic beverages and began to appreciate them (B, 208). He had always been troubled by insomnia; for the first time in his life he was able to sleep. An incredible metamorphosis had taken place within him. His alter ego, Josephine, who had been a female, a male impersonator, and a mouse had vanished into thin air. Kafka was no longer a female, a male impersonator, and a mouse. A miracle had happened and he had become an ordinary man.

Fasting has none of the theological or metaphysical connotations attributed to it by Kafka's explicators. It is closely related to Kafka's concept of food. Kafka's heroes, both human and animal, fast only because they find the food of ordinary men so distasteful that they would rather starve than eat it. The hunger artist makes an art of fasting, but he is not a genuine artist. He fasts simply because he cannot swallow the food of ordinary men—heterosexuality.

Gregor Samsa is so nauseated by the food of ordinary men that he cannot bear to smell it. He is delirious with joy when his sister brings him "animal" food. When Gregor finally refuses to eat, it is because he can no longer tolerate living in a world in which everyone finds him so loathsome. The investigating dog fasts because he, like Kafka, is an extremely discriminating sexual deviant. He demands much more than food that will appease his appetite. He desires self-fulfillment, a passionate encounter with someone whose music is just for him, who exists only for him.

Neither Kafka nor his heroes are at all singular in respect to their external appearance. Outwardly, they are completely indistinguishable from ordinary men. However, Kafka and his heroes suffer from an egregious inner imperfection. The mixture of the elements within them is radically different from that of other men, "a difference very important for the individual, insignificant for the race" (GW, 34). When Kafka first began to keep his diary in 1910, he wrote a series of fragments in which he complained about the "corruption" of his education in his childhood. In one of these entries, he described his predicament: "Externally I am a man like others, . . . But if I lacked an upper lip here, there an ear, here a rib, there a finger, . . . this would still be no adequate counterpart to my inner imperfection. This imperfection is not congenital and therefore so much the more painful to bear. For like everyone, I too have my center of gravity inside me from birth, and this not even the most foolish education could displace. This good center of gravity I still have, but to a certain extent I no longer have the corresponding body" (DI, 19). (Kafka's concept of his gravitational center is badly confused in this fragment. It is corrected several pages later in the story of "Moment of Torment," in which he states that he is "without a center" of gravity.)

Kafka seems to be saying that he was born a male and still appears to be a male from outward appearance, but, because of the corruption of his education in his childhood, his inner body and outer body no longer correspond—in short he has become a female in a male outer body. This is his inner imperfection. Kafka refuses to accept responsibility for the defect in his personality stating: "But this imperfection is not earned either, I have suffered its emergence through no fault of my own. This is why I can find nowhere within myself any repentence, much as I may seek it" (DI, 18–19).

Kafka blamed his father for his inner imperfection, but his mother came in for her share of his censure. In brutal metaphor (DF, 157) Kafka described his mother as unconsciously playing the role of a beater in a hunt—she flushed him out so that his father could annihilate him. In reaction to his father's consistent rejection of his love, Kafka suppressed his love for his father, but his suppressed love kept him in bondage until the end of his life. In one of his dreams, Kafka reports that he is holding on to the loops of his father's bathrobe while his father is maliciously leaning so far out of the window that he is in grave danger of toppling over. Kafka cannot let go of his father even though his own life is endangered. Hall and Lind observe that this dream "portrays with utmost clarity and accuracy Kafka's unbreakable tie with his father" (CHRL, 92) and point out that Kafka "revealed a deeprooted almost umbilical attachment to his father" (CHRL, 48). They also aver that, because of Kafka's consistent rejection by his father, Kafka "could not establish an identification with his father, therefore he could not become a father" (CHRL, 73).

Hall and Lind noted that Kafka expressed no castration anxiety in his dreams and hypothesized that Kafka "already felt castrated. There was nothing to fear from that side" (CHRL, 84). We agree with these authors that "Kafka accepted his castration as a *fait accompli*," but we believe that Kafka indicated symbolically within the totality of his writings that he would have been happy to relinquish his masculinity if he had been permitted to play the role of a female. We mentioned that, in one of his extremely incoherent early diary entries, Kafka reproaches his parents and the "corrupters" of his youth for having tried to make him "another person" than the one he became. He then exclaims: "I demand from their hands the person I now am" (DI, 18). We believe that Kafka is saying in this fragment that since the corrupters of his youth castrated him and deprived him of his masculinity, he demands from the hands of his castrators the right to live in the image they had created—the image of a castrated male which he associated with the image of a female.

Kafka thought of himself as an "actor" who was playing a role he was not born to play; he was impersonating a male rather than playing the role of a male. In order to play the role of a male, he would have to be reborn and reeducated. This theme appears frequently in Kafka's works. In a diary entry, Kafka describes a theater director who has to create everything from the very beginning; he has even to father his actors. He is too harrassed to admit a visitor because he is busy diapering a future actor (DII, 222). In another diary entry, he complains that in order to exist in his world, he would have to start "afresh as a baby" (DI, 43). He wrote Milena that he had not only to earn his present and his future but also had to create his past—the common heritage of all other men (M, 219). In *The Trial*, Joseph K., who is identified with Kafka, believes that in order to present his case to the court, he must recall and justify every moment of his past (T ,161). For this colossal undertaking, Kafka needed the patience of a Sisyphus. The mere thought of this endless, frustrating task filled him with impatience. Impatience was for Kafka the most heinous sin.

Because he always felt so precariously balanced, Kafka had an inordinate respect and admiration for all men who could maintain their emotional and psychosexual balance. The youthful victim in "Moment of Torment" had been precariously balanced before his seduction. In "Children on a Country Road" (PC, 21–25), Kafka describes this withdrawn, solitary child who was already deeply concerned about his gravitational center. When he rode on a swing in his father's garden, he felt, as the birds soared above him, "not that they were rising but that I was falling." "Nothing was lost" at that time, because he was on a swing when he felt this topsy-turvy sensation, and his inability to tell up from down could have been explained by the laws of nature.

This boy joins his adolescent companions, who leap into ditches, jumping up and down on each other, obviously engaging in adolescent tussles and sex play (PC, 22). When night falls, the children run home in full stride, breaking into song. The boy sings with them and thinks: "When one joins in song with others it is like being drawn on by a fish hook." Already the boy senses his deviant nature, which makes him react to the music (the normal latent homosexuality of adolescence) of his companions with pain and ecstasy. On the way home, the tired, innocent boy waits for his friends to pass the crossroad. Then, when they no longer can see where he is going, he deliberately turns off the road, heading for a city in the south which is inhabited by "queer folk." The people in that city are queer, because they never get tired and cannot sleep. In Kafka's code, only the guilty never get tired and cannot sleep. The innocent, like the officials of *The Castle*, are always tired and sleep soundly.

To conceal his inner imbalance, Kafka made an art of exhibiting his remarkable self-control and composure. He depicted himself in the figure of the trapeze artist in "First Sorrow," who spent all his days and nights practicing on a trapeze in order to become adept at the most difficult art which "humanity can achieve"—the art of controlling one's body. In this story, the trapeze artist becomes "extraordinary and unique" in his skills and finally demands a second trapeze to exhibit his consummate artistry. He ignores the fact that two trapezes would "threaten his very existence." Living on a trapeze had become a compulsion, and since life had lost all significance for him, he had become suicidal (PC, 231).

Kafka's protagonists have lost the way; they have run off the rails (PC, 50) and follow a false path (GW, 25). Signposts are meaningless for them: they point the way for ordinary men who adhere to the way of our culture. Kafka's heroes are persecuted by the Court, which encompasses all of humanity, and are declared guilty without trial because they feel a compulsion to follow a deviant path. The Judges of *The Trial* and the officials of *The Castle* condone the sexual absurdities of other men, which are "nothing but the zig-zag of dogs, whereas the master walks straight ahead, not right through the middle but precisely where the road leads" (M, 34). Kafka and his heroes cannot follow this road in their quest for sexual gratification.

Despite Kafka's frequent protestations that his deviant sexuality was the indestructible element within himself and that his wound was his sole possession, there seems little doubt that for Kafka the sole criterion for happiness was the ability to stay on the road. When Milena told Kafka that her husband deceived her "a hundred times a year, . . . his face lit up" with reverence (B, 229). Kafka wrote her: "What is the importance of his occasional [sic] 'infidelity' which isn't even infidelity, for you both remain on the same road, except that on this road he strays a little to the left? What importance has this 'infidelity' which, moreover, never stops pouring forth deepest happiness even in your deepest grief? What importance has this 'infidelity' compared to my eternal bondage?" (M, 177).

It is useless for Kafka's heroes to ask authority figures to show them the way. Policemen remain on duty all hours of the day and night to give directions to the citizens of our world, but when Kafka's bachelors ask them the way, policemen treat them as if they were mentally retarded or emotionally disturbed. They address them as "Du" rather than "Sie," as if they were speaking to children or inferiors, and tell them to "Give It Up!" (DS, 201). Then they turn away with a great sweep, "like someone who wants to be alone with his laughter." All authority figures know that there is no way for Kafka's bachelors to exist in his world.

Policemen, for Kafka, were representatives of Hell (DI, 21). Nevertheless an extremely affable policeman appears in one of Kafka's dreams. He not only gives Kafka specific directions to his fiancée's house in Berlin but also encourages him by telling him that the trip can be made in six minutes (DII, 19). This unique policeman is dressed in butler's livery and acts as politely as if

he were Kafka's servant. However, Kafka's kindly policemen exist only in his dreams and fantasies and represent
the wish-fulfillment aspects of these dreams and fantasies. In the above-mentioned dream, the very fact that
Kafka is in Berlin for the purpose of visiting his fiancée
indicates his longing to renew his citizenship in the world
by embarking on the road to marriage and heirs. All policemen in his culture were eager to direct Kafka's bachelors to that road. It is only when Kafka or his deviant
heroes ask authorities to show them the way in which
they can live in their true image in their world that they
meet with scorn and derision. Kafka did not find the way
to Felice Bauer's house despite the kindly policeman's
specific instructions. Another dream followed on the
heels of the first in which Kafka found it impossible to
lay his hands on a map of Berlin (DII, 19); therefore he
was lost. He had been led astray by a sign he had seen in
the first dream which read: "Splendors of the North."

The North had a special fascination for Kafka. Vast,
frozen wastelands like Northern Russia and China represented in Kafka's code areas in which his deviant characters, who were rebels, filthy nomads, and despoilers
of civilization, could find a haven to escape persecution.
The disgusting nomads who came from the North and
invaded the square fronting the Emperor's palace, spoke
in an incomprehensible language which sounded like the
screeching of jackdaws or kavkas, with which Kafka
overtly identified himself (PC, 145). "The Bucket
Rider," who could find no warmth on earth, and "The
Country Doctor," whose life was threatened by the
community, were doomed to wander endlessly in these
icy wastes.

Russia was not only a sanctuary where two men could
lie "together on the bunk in an embrace that often
lasted ten hours unbroken" (DII, 83), it also provided
the solitude which is a prerequisite for a writer who needs
silence and isolation. When Kafka found life with his
family intolerable, he would go out for a "Sudden Walk"
(PC, 27–28). He would then experience "so extreme a

solitude that one could only call it 'Russian.' " Peculiarly enough, this "solitude" was enhanced, if he could drop in on a male friend at this late hour. The "Splendors of the North," like Kafka's wound, were the source of his agony and his ecstasy.

Nowhere in Kafka's writings is the harrowing conflict between his need to keep the silence and his compulsion to tell the whole truth so clearly revealed as in his letters to Milena. From the beginning of his courtship of Milena, Kafka tried to tell her the whole truth about himself. He described himself as a wild animal of the forest that had been living in a labyrinthine burrow (M, 150), because he was afraid of himself and because of his "fear of people!" (M, 220–21). Rather than remain buried within his burrow, he preferred "to live on the earth as the most miserable creature" (M, 98). The road which led to Milena was, for him, fraught with danger. Like his Ape, he would have to travel an unattainable distance in order to reach her (M, 47). He pleaded with Milena not to encourage him but to let him crawl to her at his own pace (M, 47). When Milena entreated then demanded that he visit her in Vienna, he at first refused point-blank. Then he explained that he could not stand the mental strain—he was "mentally ill"; his tuberculosis was "but an overflowing" of his "mental disease" (M, 53). He promised Milena that he would divulge to her the nature of his mental disease but could not bring himself to reveal it until their relationship, which was a letter romance except for four visits, had virtually dissolved.

At that time he made another effort to reveal himself, but, because he was torn apart by his conflicting need to remain silent, he could not make himself clear, and Milena did not understand him. He wrote her: "You say, Milena, that you don't understand it. Try to understand it by calling it an illness. It's one of the many manifestations of illness which psychoanalysis believes it has uncovered. I don't call it illness and I consider the therapeutic part of psychoanalysis to be a hopeless error. All of

these so-called illnesses, sad as they may appear, are
matters of faith, efforts of souls in distress to find moor-
ings in some maternal soil" (M, 217). He then explained
that his illness, which was not an illness, manifested itself in making it impossible for him to find a mooring in
life. His ship had lost its rudder and he could not direct
it: "On my own, I can't go the way I want to go, in fact
I can't even want to go it." He deplored the fact that
he had no religious faith which might have redeemed
him (M, 219).

Although Kafka had indicated in a diary entry in 1910,
which we discussed previously, that his inner imperfection was not congenital (DI, 19), in this letter written
to Milena more than a decade later, referring to himself
in the third person, he explained that his illness pre-
existed in his nature and continued "to form his nature
(as well as his body)" (M, 218). Kafka's lacerating
courtship of Milena was conducted in an ambiance of
fear. Since he did not dare to reveal the real reason for
his fear, Kafka harped incessantly on the Jewish-question.

Kafka was deeply concerned about the plight of the
Jews in Europe at the time he was courting Milena, and
his consciousness of his Jewishness may have been ex-
acerbated by the fact that he was courting a Gentile.
However, there is no doubt that Kafka used the Jewish-
question as a smoke screen in order to conceal his real
problem. When Milena, who was then married to a Jew,
whose friends had all married Jews, who had not a trace
of bigotry in her imperious, charismatic personality, took
Kafka to task for harping on the Jewish-question, he confessed lamely: "No, you don't understand me, either,
Milena, the 'Jewish-question' was after all only a silly
joke" (M, 71).

He pointed out that Milena had taken a large step
down when she married her Jewish husband (M, 60), but
if she decided to accept his "claw-like" hand, she would
surely fall into an abyss. Their union would be of a
superhuman nature, and they would both be destroyed
(M, 111). He warned her that the "world laws and the

whole police force of Heaven" were opposed to their alliance (M, 68). He explained that he suffered from an inner imperfection which he was forced to endure, but stated that "imperfection shared by two does not have to be endured" (M, 200).

Milena misunderstood Kafka's remark about "imperfection shared by two" and thought Kafka was referring to her own human frailties. Kafka then explained exactly what he meant: "By this I hadn't intended to say anything more than: I live in my dirt, that's my business. But to drag you into it as well, that's something quite different—not only as an offence against you, this is the more incidental part. . . . The terrible thing is . . . that through you I become much more conscious of my dirt and—above all—that through it salvation becomes so much more difficult for me . . . that it's any fault of yours, Milena, is out of the question" (M, 203).

When the break finally came, Kafka confessed that the romance had been doomed from its inception: "one word of truth, one word of the inevitable truth was sufficient" (M, 202) to have destroyed it, but he had been unable to say that word. He had tried to be "sincere" and to tell Milena the whole truth, but "Sergeant-Major Perkins" was holding his hand and he could only now and then "write a word in secret" (M, 215). He had been as sincere as the prison regulations permit (M, 218), but he had not been able to "convey something unconveyable," he could not "explain something inexplicable" (M, 220). He alone was at fault: there was "too little truth on my side, still far too little truth, still mostly lies, lies from fear of myself and from fear of people! This pitcher was broken long before it went to the well. And now I'll hold my tongue, so as to stick a little to the truth. Lying is terrible, a worse mental torture doesn't exist. That is why I beg of you: Please let me be silent" (M, 220–21).

Some of Kafka's explicators, notably Paul Goodman and Erich Fromm, hypothesize that Kafka's feeling of boundless guilt may have originated in a crime he imagined he had committed. They suggest that unconsciously he may have felt guilty of death wishes toward his two brothers who died in infancy. We believe that Kafka indicated in his writings that he was well aware of the "crime" he had committed. In an enigmatic letter to Milena, Kafka attempts to confess to a crime he had committed in his youth which launched him straight into Hell: "Everything was nothing but dirt, wretched abomination, drowning in Hell, and in this respect I really stand before you like a child who has done something very bad and now it stands before its mother and cries and cries and makes a vow: I will never do it again. But it is just from all this that Fear takes its strength: 'Exactly, exactly,' it says. . . . 'he has no idea! Nothing has happened yet! Thus-he-can-still-be-saved!'" (M, 108). We hypothesize that the crime Kafka confessed to Milena, just as a child might have confessed something very bad to his mother, was committed by Kafka as a young boy, as suggested in "Moment of Torment." His fault was that he made no effort to escape although he knew that he should have run away from his seducer at any cost. This young boy had also fallen into an inferno; he, too, had made a vow never to do it again. Throughout his life, Kafka was terrified that he might be lured into temptation by forces beyond his control.

We mentioned that a large number of Kafka's images, especially in his early works, are not at all original; they occur in the dreams and fantasies of homosexuals and in the content of Rorschach tests of homosexually oriented individuals. Because of the social stigma attached to homosexuality, many homosexuals in our culture develop excessive cautiousness and suspiciousness (paranoid reactions) which do not necessarily exist in the Orient or in areas where homosexuality is tolerated. Kafka's characters manifest this reaction in some of his works. In paranoid disorders, the individual projects his homosexual or incestuous desires upon the person he loves. Unable to tolerate the unconscious guilt which overwhelms him because of his illicit desires, he denies his love and believes he is being persecuted by the individual he loves. He thinks in terms of Freud's classic formula: "I do not love him; I hate him because he persecutes me." Georg Bendemann manifests this thinking disorder in "The Judgment," which we will discuss at length later.

In *The Trial*, Joseph K. displays a penchant for making unwarranted inferences because of his delusions of persecution. When he makes his eloquent speech on his first meeting with the Court of Inquiry, he "thinks" he notices that the silent Examining Magistrate has caught someone's eye in the audience. Joseph K. reacts in a typically paranoid fashion. He makes the inference that the magistrate has given one of his hired agents a secret sign to instruct the audience either to hiss or to applaud (T, 55).

He then informs the audience that, behind his arrest, there is a great organization at work, which exists for the sole purpose of accusing innocent people of guilt and starting senseless procedures against them. This organization has at its disposal a hierarchy of the highest officials who are assisted by a retinue of servants, clerks, corrupt warders, oafish inspectors, and "perhaps even hangmen, I do not shrink from that word" (T 57).

The organization which has arrested Joseph K. and is now plotting to persecute him bears a striking resemblance to the organizations which paranoid individuals complain are plotting against them. These tormented individuals read into every casual act, gesture or word, a vast personal significance (self-reference). Because Joseph K. *thought* he saw the Examining Magistrate catch someone's eye in the audience, he inferred that he must be giving that person a secret sign. In "Description of a Struggle," the bachelor who is anticipating a homosexual diversion also misinterprets his companion's casual remarks and gestures, but on a much less malignant level. Disregarding reality and thinking only in accordance with his own fears and wishes, he becomes deeply insulted when his companion whistles a tune. When his acquaintance tells him the time, he feels he is deliberately humiliating him and demands an apology. When he winks, the bachelor believes he is suggesting an appointment or an agreement that he had forgotten (DS, 16, 18).

The homosexual bachelor, avid for the love of his new acquaintance, ascribes his passion to his new friend and engages in a reverie in which he imagines his acquaintance telling his fiancée about the encounter and informing her of his infatuation with the bachelor. After imagining this scene, the bachelor, who is humiliated because his acquaintance is completely unresponsive, projects his humiliation upon his acquaintance. He realizes that if his friend made such an indiscreet confession, he would be acknowledging his homosexual orientation and would be extremely humiliated. Fantasy merges with reality in the disordered mind of the bachelor, and he thinks the whole scene has already taken place and his friend is deeply humiliated. He then thinks: "And I didn't spare my acquaintance . . . the smallest fraction of the humiliation he must have felt at making such a speech" (DS, 22).

"Description of a Struggle" is a case study in homosexual imagery and paranoid thinking, rife with concepts and images commonly seen by homosexuals on projective tests of personality. In this story, Kafka describes such blatant homosexual concepts as: a man riding another man as if he were riding a horse; a man contorting himself into peculiar postures to attract the attention of his partner (homosexual posturings); a man who fears he will be stabbed (homosexually assaulted) by another man yet makes no effort to escape. He remains for some time on the scene, hopefully and fearfully awaiting his murder (DS, 28). Two hundred feet from the "imminent murder," one of Kafka's rare kindly policemen glides along on the pavement, oblivious to what is going on. This unobservant policeman represents the wish-fulfillment aspect of this fantasy, signifying that the homosexual bachelor is free to indulge himself in his diversions—no authority figure is watching.

Scattered throughout Kafka's works are descriptions

of men sneaking up on other men; attacks from the rear; spikes driven into men's heads, necks, or backs; men being stabbed in the back or neck by other men; and men wrestling with other men. All of these images are typical of the responses given by homosexually oriented individuals on projective tests. When Kafka's bachelors engage in heterosexual interactions, they perform in filthy surroundings and manifest no pleasure in their frenzied contortions. In *The Castle*, K. and Frieda lie on a barroom floor in puddles of beer, or they perform in view of witnesses who may possibly be used to attest to K.'s virility or his heterosexuality.

Knives, daggers, bayonets, and guns are common sexual symbols, but in Kafka's literary creations they are used only by men in order to "attack" other men. The writer of a manifesto issued to his fellow-lodgers tries to dispose of his toy rifles which are broken and useless (DF, 55). These toy rifles are the inseparable companions of the two bouncing balls which disturb Mr. Blumfeld, although they are his "true companions in life." Despite their childish good nature, K. consistently abuses the two assistants who have been sent to him by the authorities of *The Castle*. He finds them such a nuisance that he finally discharges them. Charles Neider identified these assistants as testicles. We suggest that Mr. Blumfeld's bouncing balls and the warders of *The Trial* are their counterparts. The warders inform Joseph K. that he is arrested (psychologically) and tell him that they are required to guard him ten hours a day (T, 9–10). They stand closer to him "than any other people in the world" (T, 9); in fact they stand so close to him that the "belly of the second warder . . . kept butting against him in an almost friendly way" (T, 7).

"Description of a Struggle" depicts the panic which must have engulfed Kafka after he had experienced his "Moment of Torment." It is the description of the panic experienced by a latent homosexual when he first discovers his deviant orientation. The panic lasts until the person decides whether or not to accept his illicit drives.

There is little doubt that Kafka rejected these drives, as did the bachelor in "Moment of Torment," but for him this was no solution. His expulsion from Paradise haunted him forever. His torment was "everlasting" because he could not renounce his citizenship in his world, nor could he renounce the ecstasy he had experienced in this encounter.

In "Description of a Struggle," Kafka portrays himself in two roles: he is the bachelor who is unable to renounce his homosexual drives; he is also the new acquaintance who struggles to prove his heterosexuality by endlessly kissing the ladies. The homosexual bachelor is identified with Kafka, the writer, by the coat he is wearing. Kafka's writer images share his yellow, well-worn coat of shreds and patches, which resemble Kafka's yellowed, shredded and patched manuscripts. The bachelor still attends parties, but he is alienated from normal men and women and sits alone at a wobbly, three-legged table symbolizing his own instability. The acquaintance, who is frantically trying to assume a heterosexual role, has become a veritable Don Juan. Kafka's divided self is revealed by the total lack of communication between these two figures. Neither has any understanding of the other; it is impossible for them to keep in step with each other. Within this homosexual fantasy, Kafka describes in graphic images the gamut of delusions, projections, ideas of reference, hallucinations, and the magical thinking of a person who is experiencing a homosexual panic.

The homosexual bachelor has fallen deeply in love with his new male acquaintance of several minutes' standing. He is not jealous of the girls this Don Juan is always kissing and has no objections to their kissing his beloved—it is their duty to kiss and caress him, "but they mustn't carry him off. . . . But if they carry him off, then they steal him from me. And he must always remain with me. . . . Suppose some jealous man . . . attacks him? What will happen to me? Am I to be just kicked out of the world? . . . No, he won't get rid of me" (DS, 20).

The homosexual bachelor in "Description of a Struggle" is looking forward to a homosexual encounter, but he soon realizes that his companion is completely unresponsive. He contorts himself into bizarre postures to attract the attention of his companion, but his acquaintance does not understand the meaning of his homosexual posturings and bluntly tells him to straighten up. At times, as is usual in Kafka's early incoherent narratives, the two aspects of the self blend into a single image. The acquaintance has delusions of bodily separation: his hands dangle gaily in his cuffs. They are not under his control and act as if the left hand does not know what the right hand is doing (DS, 24). When he tells the bachelor of this remarkable happening, the bachelor finds it difficult to restrain himself from kissing him on his eyes (DS, 24).

The homosexual bachelor has delusions of bodily change: his legs grow so long that they cover the landscape, making a bridge by means of which he can escape to another world (DS, 87). His arms grow so huge that they crush his head, which has become infinitesimal, no larger than an ant's head, signifying the diminution of his ego. The "slightly damaged" crushed head is a delusion of bodily disfigurement and bodily injury. The arms and hands that crush the head to a pulp touch an iron signpost—the only solid object in the midst of the bachelor's dissolving world. Only when the bachelor is free of conscious control (symbolized by the crushed head) can his body find its true direction and pursue its own ends.

The bachelor has delusions of bodily movement: he feels as if he were being projected into space and people are floating about him (DS, 65). He swims on the pavement (DS, 32) and becomes seasick on dry land (DS, 60). He has delusions of unreality: nothing is real. People consist of sumptuous dresses; houses are merely portals; the sky has clouds glued onto it in the shape of hearts (DS, 82). He has delusions of world disintegration: high houses collapse for no apparent reason (DS, 63); "things sink away like fallen snow" around him, "whereas for other people even a little liquor glass stands on the table steady as a statue" (DS, 62). People fall dead in the streets and are hidden in shopkeeper's warehouses, just as Gregor Samsa was secreted by his father (ch. 5). He has delusions of nihilism: he is a nothing, a nobody who wants to go on an excursion to the mountains with his fellow nobodies, because when nobodies get together, "their throats become free and they can break into song." Since "song" for Kafka was a euphemism for homosexual interactions, in this passage Kafka indicates his desire to go on a homosexual orgy with his fellow deviants (nobodies) to the mountains, where he will feel free to break into song.

The bachelor has delusions of dehumanization: eight Russian wolfhounds are Parisian dandies in disguise (DS, 79). He has delusions of grandeur and engages in magical thinking. Since the world has become meaningless for him and he can no longer live in it, he builds up a megalomaniacal world of his own to inflate his infinitesimal ego and travels through a mad world of his own creation. He transforms himself into a "small bird on a twig," assuming the image Kafka often used to identify himself, a kavka or a raven (DS, 38).

However the bachelor has not yet slipped over the razor-edge of sanity; he therefore suddenly realizes that he is not omnipotent—he has forgotten to cause the moon to rise. The world he has created in his fancy disintegrates before his eyes. He has hallucinatory sensations: he hears sobs from afar and does not realize it is he who is crying because it is impossible for him to escape from his suffering (DS, 43). He recalls his childhood Paradise, where everything was beautiful. People said and did ordinary, commonplace things as if they were living in an ordinary, commonplace world. Everything was beautiful then, not because it was so beautiful but because it was not the terrible inferno in which he is now living. Every commonplace memory of the world of his childhood strikes him with amazement, because for him the ordinary has become a miracle (J, 74).

In another episode of this narrative, Kafka identifies himself with a fat man who is all intellect. He is so lacking in substance that a gnat flies right through his body. The fat man mirrors Kafka in that he, too, cannot accept the nature of ordinary men. He closes his eyes to the nature (landscape) of the world because his nature blocks him from "attaining the attainable" (DS, 45).

The world of the nature of ordinary men forces him to open his eyes and admire it, but this he cannot do. Hypocritically he tries to praise the nature of other men, but it is against his instincts to do this. He cannot keep his eyes open to nature. Finally, after shouting paeans of praise to a nature that he abhors, he can no longer maintain his self-deception and cries: "I implore you—mountain, flowers, grass, bush and river, give me some room so that I may breathe." He cannot breathe in the world of ordinary men. Kafka, who referred to his tuberculosis as the symbol of his deepest wound, was also unable to breathe in his world.

The fat man, who delivers a long monologue while he is drowning, knows that he is lost. Nature is avenging itself upon him because he insisted on closing his eyes to it. He has been blind to the world of other men and deaf to its music. He has attacked the nature of other men by creating his own music. Like the performing dogs (GW, 15), he committed an abomination by creating his own cacaphonous music (ch. 3).

Since Kafka was never able to forget or annihilate any experience, he may have recalled the images and symbols which occurred to him in his homosexual panic and used them later in his creative works. He told Janouch: "What is written is merely the dregs of the experience. . . . Art is always a matter of the entire personality. For that reason it is fundamentally tragic" (J, 46). Kafka's images, structures, and techniques emanated from his entire personality which was governed by his deviant sexual drives. The technique of separating the different aspects of the self and thinking of them as completely different individuals is characteristic of certain types of disturbed individuals. Many authors have used the device of depicting the self as two different individuals, but Kafka depicts his divided self consistently in a great number of his narratives. In "The Judgment," Kafka dissects himself into three distinct individuals in deadly conflict with each other. In other narratives, Kafka depicts dreamlike images, each of which represents some aspect of himself or his problem.

Kafka shares with his fellow-deviants their most distinctive trait: their simultaneous need to conceal themselves and to exhibit themselves. Many of Kafka's characters are exhibitionists: the trapeze artist, the equestrienne, the humanized ape, and Josephine, the Singer. Even "The Hunger Artist" needs an audience to watch him starve to death. The difficulty homosexuals experience in relating to ordinary people and identifying with them is reflected in Kafka's choice of singular and eccentric characters. They are bohemians, tricksters, nobodies, mechanical men like "Oradek" (PC, 160), men who are merely numbers like his "Eleven Sons" (PC, 161) and his twelve undifferentiated miners (PC, 155). They are puppetlike acrobats like his equestrienne who rides endlessly on the merry-go-round of life into a drab future with only one spectator in the audience aware of her torment (PC, 144); or his trapeze artist who spends his lifetime exhibiting his remarkable skills in body control. They are social outcasts like Barnabas's family in *The Castle*, or the land surveyor, who may be an imposter. The land he set out to reapportion cannot be measured; it exists beyond the frontiers of civilization. There is no proof that he was ever called to *The Castle*.

Kafka's distaste for his aberrant sexuality led him to identify himself with the disgusting nomads and barbarians who befoul civilization. His difficulty with his animal drives led him to identify himself with numerous animals, from the most wild and violent to the most tame and timid. He was careful to cage his beautiful, wild animals. Kafka overtly identified himself with a raven, saying "I am a jackdaw—a *kavka* . . . my wings are atrophied. . . . I hop about bewildered among my fellow men. They regard me with deep suspicion. And indeed I am a dangerous bird" (J, 16–17). When he began to achieve his psychosexual balance, he identified himself with a sparrow so timid that it refused to eat food that was offered to it (M, 55).

We mentioned that many homosexuals develop excessive fears and become unduly secretive and suspicious. They think people are always watching them. Old persons represent the authority figures which threaten them. Kafka and his heroes are terrified of slander. "A Little Woman" is one of Kafka's extremely rare characters who existed in reality outside of Kafka's family. She was Kafka's landlady at the time when he became sufficiently balanced psychosexually so that he could live with Dora Dymant. Kafka was terrified of this little woman. He knew she was suspicious of him and feared she would denounce him and ruin him. He was then living as a solid citizen and was fearful that this sharp-witted woman would recognize him (PC, 239). Kafka and Dora moved away from her house after six weeks (B, 197).

In a number of Kafka's narratives, people are always watching. In "Description of a Struggle," people watch the odd couple who are night-walking. Joseph K.'s arrest is witnessed by people looking through their windows. He is deeply concerned when he discovers that two employees at the bank are witnesses to his arrest; yet in his ambivalence, he waits up all hours to inform Fräulein Bürstner of his arrest, acting out the details in a most exhibitionistic fashion. To demonstrate his innocence, he seizes her, kissing her "all over the face, like some thirsty animal lapping greedily at a spring of long-sought fresh water" (T, 38). He becomes furious when Frau Grubach casts aspersions on Fräulein Bürstner's character by saying: "I try to keep my house respectable," and shouts: "if you want to keep your house respectable you'll have to begin by giving me notice" (T, 29).

Despite their projection of blame upon others, homosexuals are frequently guilt-ridden. Kafka's characters insist that they are blameless, yet they are generally filled with guilt or shame. Although Kafka believed he had exorcized the spectre of his guilt in writing "The Judgment," his letters to Milena indicate that he remained guilt-ridden every time he thought seriously of marriage. Joseph K., who protests throughout his trial that he is innocent, is filled with boundless "shame" because of his pusillanimous submission to the corrupt authorities who condemn him to death.

3

Investigations of a Dog

The story of the homosexual encounter, "Moment of Torment," which had been described so incoherently in his diary, obsessed Kafka throughout his lifetime, clamoring for artistic expression. Five times between November 1910 and August 1911, Kafka tried to rewrite this story but his efforts proved fruitless. We believe that Kafka attempted a sixth version in 1915 and abandoned it because it did not meet with his perfectionist standards; then toward the end of his life, still obsessed by the story of his homosexual awakening, Kafka evolved the final form of this story in "Investigations of a Dog" (DII, 114). The emotional tenor in this exquisite narrative is subdued, and the style is that of Kafka at the very peak of his artistic powers.

Simply by dehumanizing the bachelor, a procedure which had proved so successful in "The Metamorphosis," Kafka appears to be telling a completely different story. The truth of the homosexual encounter is concealed in endless obfuscations and by the use of his code, but the basic facts about the homosexual awakening remain the same. Kafka deliberately places his narrating dog (who is his inner image) in dogdom, because he is leading a dog's life (DI, 23).

In this story, the dog has an apocalyptic experience during which he loses his childhood innocence and comes to the realization that he is a sexual deviant. The incident must have happened early in the dog's youth because he says, "it robbed me of a great part of my childhood" (GW, 20). The dog had from his earliest days recognized that he was peculiar. He says: "from the very beginning, I sensed some discrepancy, some little maladjustment" (GW, 3). Wilhelm Emrich translates this passage: "I sensed a spot where there was a small crack" (E, 181), the small crack corresponding to the invisible ulcer which had erupted during the homosexual awakening in "Moment of Torment." The dog's "maladjustment" manifested itself in causing him to cringe with fear, helpless embarrassment, and even despair when a male dog in his circle whom he liked merely took a look at him.

Despite his blemish, in outer appearance the dog seemed to be an ordinary dog that was indistinguishable from other dogs in the canine community. He says: "I am at bottom, then, no different from any other dog. . . . Only the mixture of the elements is different, a difference very important for the individual, insignificant for the race" (GW, 33–34). "I am neither particularly exceptional in any way, nor particularly repellent in any way . . . the only strange thing about me is my nature, yet even that, as I am always careful to remember, has its foundations in universal dog nature" (GW, 40). The dog thus identifies himself with ordinary dogs, saying that the only difference between him and his fellows is an imbalance in the mixture of the elements within himself, a difference which is meaningless for the race but of the greatest possible significance for himself. It was the imbalance of the mixture of the elements within himself that created his peculiar "nature," which caused him to stray from the path of ordinary dogs to an opposite path, which originally had been paved by our first fathers, who, when they strayed, did not realize that their "aberration was to be an endless one" (GW, 47).

Up to the time that this dog experienced his homosexual awakening, he did not believe that he was at all different from ordinary dogs in any of the essential aspects of dog behavior. All dogs, whatever their species, looked like dogs to him. It was his innocence of good and evil that was responsible for his remaining on the spot when he witnessed an extraordinary exhibition of a group of musical performing dogs. Only after witnessing their astounding performance, did the thought occur to him that "Perhaps they were not dogs at all?" (GW, 13), but ignorant as he was of the facts of life, he intuitively realized that all dogs, even deviant ones, are members of the canine race, and he reassured himself on that score, saying "But how should they not be dogs?"

Just before his encounter with the musical dogs, the dog had been running about for some time in a state of blissful exaltation when suddenly he had a feeling that he had arrived at the right place and came to an abrupt stop. He saw before him seven performing musical dogs that were making an unearthly concatenation of sounds. The dog, like the bachelor in "Moment of Torment," did not run away. He stayed because he thought that the dogs were ordinary dogs. If he had not seen distinctly that they were dogs and that they were responsible for the cacophonic music which was emanating from them, he would have run away, "but as it was" he stayed.

For the first time in his life, the dog heard a piercing, terrible kind of music which seemed to be directed at his total being. He had never paid any attention to music before; therefore he was completely astonished at the effect that this devastating music was having on him. He became breathless and howled as if he were in excruciating pain (GW, 11). The music leaped out at him from all directions, and when a respite came, for he had been practically swooning, he asked the dogs what they were doing. The dogs did not answer his question. Then the music started again, and the dog felt its impact again. He says, "it robbed me of my wits, whirled me around in its circles as if I myself were one of the musicians instead of being only their victim" (GW, 12). The dog, like his counterpart in "Moment of Torment" thus became a victim because he was completely overpowered by the music of these performing dogs.

When the dog momentarily regained his senses, he became aware that these musical dogs were breaking the law and began to wonder whether they were dogs at all. Even though they were remarkable musicians, "the law was valid for them too." He knew this with certainty even though he was a "child." He knew too that these dogs were doing what is considered to be the most indecent thing in dogdom: they were walking on their hind legs, exposing their nakedness. Moreover, they were doing this as if it were "a meritorious act," and when, for whatever reason, they "let their front paws fall, they were literally appalled as if at an error, as if Nature were an error, hastily raised their legs again, and their eyes seemed to be begging for forgiveness for having been forced to cease momentarily from their abomination" (GW, 15).

By this time the dog lost his gravitational center, just as the bachelor in "Moment of Torment" had lost his. His world had turned topsy-turvy, as if it were standing on its head. He could not believe what he was seeing and began to wonder where he was and what could have happened to him. The dog then decided, that even though he was a child, he must reprove these dogs, make them aware of the sin they were committing, and stop them from committing further sin. However, before he could get to his feet, the music started again, and he was so overwhelmed that he could not move a step. By this time he could no longer admonish the musical dogs and no longer wanted to instruct them. For his part, they could go right on committing sin and "seducing others to the sin" of watching them (GW, 16). Later on, after the concert was over and the dogs had dispersed, the dog tried to rationalize the behavior of these dogs that had acted so strangely that he questioned their very doggishness. He could not bring himself to condemn them, saying, "If it was a sin, well it was a sin" (GW, 17). However, he regretted the loss of his innocence and blamed his parents for letting him run around so freely (GW, 18).

After having related this remarkable experience, the pedantic dog began to quibble about this concert. At one time he implied that he might have "conjured up" this performance; at another time he stated firmly that he saw the dog musicians with his own eyes (GW, 35). Whether he conjured them up or really saw them is irrelevant because he finally admits that it all began with this concert. He no longer blames the concert because he realizes that it was his "innate disposition" that had driven him on, and it would soon have found another opportunity for "coming into action" if this concert had not taken place (GW, 19).

The dog, who had been transported by the music of the deviant dogs, was as confused as he was ecstatic and could not understand what had happened. Being a dog, he had been a witness to heterosexual activities from early infancy. Music had surrounded him as a commonplace, ordinary, and indispensable element of existence, and his parents had referred to it when necessary and had subtly instructed him in a manner suitable to a child's understanding. Yet, young as he was, he realized that the performance of the musical dogs was different: it was a sin and an abomination. The dog seems to be well acquainted with Leviticus and seems to have known that the law firmly states: "Thou shalt not lie with mankind, as with womankind: it *is* an abomination." He may also have been aware that, in chapters 18 and 20 of Leviticus, only homosexuality is termed an "abomination"; all other sexual offences are called "defilements," "corruption," or "iniquities."

One might say that the dog had paid no attention to the music in his environment (heterosexual activity), because he was too young; he was not in a state of readiness and could not have responded to it. But Kafka implies that he was in a state of readiness; he had been "led by a vague desire" and when he came to a stop, he knew he was in the right place. One might also say that what the dog witnessed was a heterosexual encounter because he was in a state of readiness for the first time. But this is impossible, because heterosexual activity was so much a part of the natural life of the dog that he would never have thought of questioning it and would never have thought of it as an "abomination." It was because his experience was so incredible and so foreign to his comprehension that he felt compelled to question every dog he met about this strange occurrence.

In the context of this story it seems clear that the music of the performing dogs means complete sexual gratification of a deviant nature; a breakthrough to the total being of the narrating dog whose nature was different from that of ordinary dogs and who therefore responded to a different kind of sexual gratification. If there is any doubt that the spectacle the dog witnessed was a homosexual orgy, that doubt is dispelled at the end of the story. The dog finally succumbs to a beautiful male hunter dog whose music seems to exist just for his sake. After the dog experiences this apotheosis, he joins the ranks of the silent because he feels that such things cannot be told.

The dog had just emerged from puppyhood when he experienced his first homosexual encounter. He was so excited and confused that he could not contain himself. Although he knew intuitively that the dogs had been committing a sin, he could not repress his curiosity and pestered all the dogs in his circle with questions. All the dogs he questioned tried to "stop up" his mouth (GW, 25), every dog tried to divert him "almost lovingly from a false path." Now that the dog is older, he knows exactly what they were doing. They wanted "to divert me from my path. They did not succeed; they achieved the opposite" (GW, 25–26). The dog no longer blames them because he realizes that no one on earth could have set him on the right path; he was predisposed to taking a wrong path because of his wound, he went astray because of his nature; the mixture of the elements within him was different (GW, 33–34); therefore he had a different sexual orientation.

In this story, Kafka seems to be trying to explain why

he never declared himself openly, why he felt compelled to remain silent. He must have fancied himself in the role of the investigating dog, who, frustrated and resentful because he could obtain no answers to his questions and crushed by the silence of his fellow-dogs, delivers an eloquent soliloquy in which he wonders whether he should exhort his fellow-dogs to speak up once and for all and shatter the oppressive silence. He says: "Now one might say, 'you torment yourself because of your fellow-dogs, because of their silence on crucial questions; you assert that they know more than they admit, more than they will allow to be valid, and that this silence, the mysterious reason for which is also, of course, tacitly concealed, poisons existence and makes it unendurable for you so that you must either alter it or have done with it; that may be, but you are yourself a dog, you have also the dog knowledge; well, bring it out, not merely in the form of a question, but as an answer. If you utter it, who will think of opposing you? The great choir of dogdom will join in as if it had been waiting for you. Then you will have clarity, truth, avowal, as much of them as you desire. The roof of this wretched life, of which you say so many hard things, will burst open, and all of us, shoulder to shoulder, will ascend into the lofty realm of freedom. And if we should not achieve that final consummation, if things should become worse than before, if the whole truth should be more insupportable than the half, if it should be proved that the silent are in the right as the guardians of existence, if the faint hope that we still possess should give way to complete hopelessness, the attempt is still worth the trial, since you do not desire to live as you are compelled to live" (GW, 27–28). The narrating dog then admits that he cannot reproach his colleagues because they remain silent; he is just as silent as they are, "dour out of fear" (GW, 29).

Both Kafka and the narrating dog wanted to break the silence so that there could be clarity and truth—instead of truth with no vestige of clarity because the truth had to be masked, disguised, or concealed. The dog's greatest need was to "achieve truth and escape from this world of falsehood" (GW, 70); to remove his mask and appear in his own image, to claim his right to exist and to nourish himself sexually according to his needs. But neither Kafka nor his spokesman, the narrating dog, could speak up and break the silence. The dog had relinquished all hope of speaking up since he had become an adult.

The dog then avers that he shares not only his "ever-desirous flesh" with his colleagues; he shares the key to their knowledge as well, but this key he cannot possess except in common with all others. Finally he reveals why throughout his lifetime he has refrained from convoking a meeting in which all deviant dogs could have assembled in order to pool their knowledge so that they might arrive at the "marrow" of the truth. After much thought, he had come to the conclusion that the "truth is a poison." Although he did not subscribe to the laws of his forefathers, he did not dare to change them because those laws were based on sources which were no longer definable. He had become convinced that the "silent are in the right as the guardians of existence." To tell the truth might cause the foundations of our civilization to crumble.

As the investigating dog grew older, he realized that his first shattering experience with the performing dogs had been so remarkable, not because it was a breakthrough to the dog's awareness of his deviant sexuality for, if this encounter had not taken place, another encounter was imminent (GW, 19), but because the dog had witnessed it through the eyes of a child (GW, 16). Now that he is older, he has seen other varieties of dogs that are just as peculiar. One breed, of which he has heard but which he has never seen, is the soaring dog, a dog that hovers "in the air, and that is all . . . someone now and then refers to art and artists, but there it ends." These soaring dogs, who have voluntarily relinquished their lives on earth and have chosen to live an empty life up in the air, have presented an insoluble enigma to Kafka's exegetes.

Kafka's interpreters have failed to identify these dogs because they were not aware that Kafka was indulging himself in irony in his portrayal of this species. Kafka's description of these dogs gives the clue to their identity. They are no larger than a kavka, they fly in the air like kavkas, they are hybrids like Kafka, they engage in profound, philosophical meditations like Kafka, and they are artists like Kafka: in short the soaring dog is Kafka. It is sometimes extremely difficult to detect Kafka's corrosive irony, but the narrating dog gave the clue to the identification of these dogs by his sanctimonious condemnation of this species. Suddenly, for no apparent reason, the gentle, tolerant, philosophical, narrating dog became tartuffian in his bigotry and his vehement censure of this deviant species.

The scathing denunciation of the soaring dog by the narrating dog is an example of Kafka's elusive irony, which he frequently used as a technique for confusing his readers. In this story, he compounded the confusion by using a device which he had used previously in "The Judgment," which we shall discuss in the next chapter. He depicted his divided self as two distinctly delineated individuals in deadly conflict with each other and completely alienated from each other. Kafka had created the original mystification by dehumanizing himself and assuming the role of the narrating dog who represented his inner self. He then put his paintbrush in the paw of the investigating dog and permitted him to depict his outer image—the image of Kafka, the writer and the artist. Naturally, the investigating dog would never have been able to visualize Kafka's outer image because the various aspects of the self are alien to each other and incapable of recognizing each other even though they may be aware of each other's existence. The narrating dog was aware of Kafka's existence and knew that Kafka played an important role in his life, but, since he could not conceive of Kafka's outer image, he painted him in the only image he knew—a foppish, birdlike, hybrid dog, no bigger than a kavka, the bird with which Kafka always identified himself (J, 16).

The investigating dog has nothing but contempt for Kafka whom he describes as a "weedy, brushed and curled fop" (GW, 34), who, like all of Kafka's homosexual protagonists, has withdrawn from the good earth and the general life of the community. The kavka-dog lives in an ivory tower and is always absorbed in his occupations, always engaged in profound thought, and always so immersed in his philosophical meditations that he cannot tear himself away from his labors. The narrating dog finds the kavka-dog unendurably boring. He thinks his reflections are sheer nonsense because they are the observations of an ivory-towered scholar who has both feet firmly planted in midair. He thinks his entire life is purposeless and meaningless, and, since the kavka-dog is obligated to remain silent on his problem and his secret, he calls his existence a "dumb senselessness" (GW, 35–36). Despite his virulent criticism, the investigating dog is greatly impressed by the kavka-dog's techniques and cannot refrain from admiring them. For him, all of the kavka-dog's creative works are merely a technical accomplishment because since the kavka-dog has only one theme—the plight of a homosexual in his culture—he must concentrate on developing technical devices which will permit him to use that theme over and over again so that no one will discover his dearth of subject matter or his techniques of obfuscation.

The narrating dog observes that the kavka species "must do what they can to obtain pardon, and not openly—that would be a violation of the obligation to keep silence—they must do what they can to obtain pardon for their way of life, or else divert attention from it so that it may be forgotten—and they do this . . . by means of an almost unendurable volubility. They are perpetually talking, partly of their philosophical reflections, . . . partly of the observations which they have made from their exalted stations" (GW, 37). The exasperating volubility of the kavka-dog cannot be construed to mean oral glibness, because this species is "invariably seen alone" (GW, 39). It refers to their reflections and meditations which link them to Kafka. The compulsion of the kavka-dogs to pray for pardon sheds light on one of Kafka's most cryptic and most frequently misinterpreted diary entries in which Kafka characterizes writing "as a form of prayer" (B, 78). Max Brod misled future expositors by explaining that Kafka, who in Brod's opinion, was well on the road to becoming a saint (B, 49), was striving to achieve the quintessence of purity and perfection in his life as well as in his art.

There is no doubt that Kafka worked ceaselessly to achieve perfection in his work, but the predicament of the kafka-dogs emphatically contradicts Brod's interpretation. These kavka-dogs have obviously committed a transgression of such a nature that they must forever keep it a secret. They must seek to obtain pardon for this sin, "and not openly—that would be a violation of the obligation to keep silence." It appears, then, that Kafka may have considered his writing to be a form of prayer to obtain pardon for whatever homosexual practices in which he indulged, and not openly, because he was compelled by the mores of his culture to keep silent; or to divert attention from his way of life so that it might be forgotten.

The investigating dog wonders why the kavka-dog floats in the air (GW, 36). The kavka-dog has long since lost his gravitational center. He has no roots on earth and is not attracted to the earth—therefore he floats in the air. He has detached himself from the nourishing earth because it did not provide him with the nourishment he needed. He has retired to the solitude of his ivory tower to write because writing is his sole source of nourishment even though it does not sustain him. The kavka breed of dogs have let "their legs, the pride of dogs, fall into desuetude" (GW, 36); actually Kafka had let his entire body fall into decay. At the time this story was written, Kafka was suffering from tuberculosis. He

welcomed his affliction because it would release him
from earth. Because of his disease, he takes lengthy rest
cures during which he is free to concentrate on his writing. He is "reaping without having sowed," and is being
provided for at the "cost of the community" (GW, 36).
He lives on a tiny pension supplemented in times of acute
distress by tokens of material help from his family, who
are eager to offer him much more, but he is proud and
refuses to accept it. The kavka-dog is always resting on
cushions, concerned primarily with his comfort. Kafka
is resting on cushions in various sanatoria, or wherever
he can be taken care of, and is now "particularly de-
pendent" upon his fellowmen because he is in the terminal stage of tuberculosis. The narrating dog, who is filled
with a zest for life, cannot understand how it is possible
for any dog to give up "life on solid ground" voluntarily
to live in the air "merely for the sake of comfort and a
certain technical accomplishment" (GW, 39), and cannot understand why the kavka-dog is so obsessed by his
labors. Kafka was so engrossed in his writing that he
edited "Josephine the Singer, or the Mouse Folk" on his
deathbed.

The investigating dog finds the kavka-dog so feeble
that he wonders contemptuously if he is capable of propagation; has he "actually the strength for that?" (GW,
38–39). He observes that even if the kavka-dog could
propagate, which is most unlikely, he has no opportuni-
ties to indulge himself. His breed is always seen alone.
He wonders why the kavka species has not become ex-
tinct because this variety of dogs do not seem to "multi-
ply by propagation," yet it is a fact that the kavka species
is always in evidence (GW, 39–40). In one way or another they manage to meet their colleagues somewhere,
and in some fashion they seem able to "conjure generations of themselves out of nothingness" (GW, 40–41).
Here Kafka explains his recurrent theme of the eternal
aspect of his problem, which he depicts in "The Hunter
Gracchus." It is an old, old, story, known by all of the
historians of the past. Homosexuality has existed from

time immemorial and will continue to exist until the end of time.

When the narrating dog asks other dogs what the kavka-dog is doing, they tell him he is making a contribution to knowledge. One or another dog invariably objects and says that the kavka-dog's contributions are worthless; the reply to that is a "shrug, or a change of the subject, or annoyance, or laughter" (GW, 38), as if the kavka-dog were engaged in some obscene or unmentionable activity. Generally, however, most dogs agree that the kavka-dog is contributing to knowledge, and finally the investigating dog accepts this consensus, saying with ironic detachment: "And perhaps indeed it is well not to be too obstinate, but to yield to public sentiment, to accept the extant soaring dogs, and without recognizing their right to existence, which cannot be done, yet to tolerate them. But more than this must not be required; that would be going too far, and yet the demand is made" (GW, 38).

As the investigating dog grew older, he became less scornful and critical of the kavka-dog; in fact he achieved a sort of synthesis with him and merged into his image. He became a recluse, removed himself from the life of the community and began to work on his hopeless but, as far as he was concerned, "indispensable" investigations (GW, 4). However in his early days the investigating dog was no recluse. When he started his researches, his first questions were concerned with food (Kafka's code word for sexual gratification), because his "main object" was to achieve "practical results" (GW, 76). He was a young dog with a splendid appetite and he had to find out where and how he could obtain sexual gratification. His researches have a fuzzy quality because he is trying to confuse the reader by not asking "genuine questions." He rationalizes his evasiveness, explaining: "One question sounds like another"; besides, sometimes dogs ask questions as if "they were trying to obliterate every trace of the genuine questions" (GW, 42). His first question: "On what does the canine race nourish itself?"

(GW, 20), is disposed of immediately. He accepts the obvious answer given by the majority of the dog community: "food" (GW, 21–22). He also knows that all nourishing food is to be found on earth. All one has to do is to water the ground and scratch, or cultivate and water the soil. Then food will be forthcoming in various qualities, quantities, and in various ways, places, and hours (GW, 21–23). Some religious dogs engage in incantations to hasten the arrival of food, but he is not one of them. He believes in natural science, which teaches that all food comes from the earth, and although science has no objection to the religious rituals and incantations of those who look to heaven for food, he disagrees with the scientists, saying, "I simply cannot conceive how the learned can bear to let our people, unruly and passionate as they are, chant their incantations" to the heavens (GW, 55).

He confesses that the second question: "Whence does the earth procure this food?" is not a genuine question, saying: "For instance when I asked: 'Whence does the earth procure this food' was I troubled . . . about the earth; was I troubled about the labors of the earth? Not in the least; that, as I very soon recognized, was far from my mind; all I cared for was the race of dogs, that and nothing else" (GW, 26).

His fellow-dogs were not at all confused by this question. They were annoyed and embarrassed because they realized that what the dog was actually asking was where was it possible for a deviant dog to get sexual satisfaction? Was there nourishment for him on this earth or did he have to starve until he could attain satisfaction in Heaven? Since the lusty dog had no faith, he was not concerned with heavenly nourishment; his only concern was where could he find dogs of his species on earth. His question actually was: "But where, then, are my real colleagues?" He freely admits this saying: "that is the burden of my complaint, that is the kernel of it. Where are they? Everywhere and nowhere. Perhaps my next-door neighbor . . . is one of them. Is he my real col-

league? I do not know" (GW, 43). The narrating dog
wants to ask his neighbor if he is one of his species, but
he does not dare to ask him (GW, 49). Then he wonders if he disappoints his neighbor, just as his neighbor
disappoints him, by not asking.

The investigating dog's scientific researches were de-
signed to discover ways of procuring homosexual satisfaction without endangering his position in the community. It was therefore essential that the food come to
him; he could not risk his reputation by going out to
hunt for it. He performed various intricate experiments
to see if he could attract food to him from any direction,
and to his great surprise, he discovered that food sometimes pursues the hungry. For a time he was very happy,
but his happiness was short-lived because a "stir of curiosity ran through" his neighborhood, he "attracted uneasy attention" (GW, 58). Nevertheless, when he was
ravenous, he "swallowed down the tempting food"
(GW, 58), but he was overwhelmed by guilt and fear
when he did this. He says: "I . . . felt outlawed in my
innermost heart and had run my head against the tra-
ditional walls of my species like a savage" (GW, 63).

Unable to bear the burden of his guilt and fear, he
resolved to conduct an experiment in fasting, recording
his findings for the benefit of science. He felt that he
would redeem himself by fasting. He would then be
completely accepted by the dog community who would
ride him on their shoulders with great honor and give
him the warmth that he yearned for so deeply. Several
of his predecessors had established precedents for fasting: the hunger artist and Gregor Samsa had maintained
their fasts until they starved to death. After consulting
our sages and learning that the majority of commentators approve freely of fasting (GW, 66), the investigating dog began his first great fast—a fast so debilitating
that he has not yet recovered although he is long past
adulthood. At the height of his powers, when his sexual
appetite was so splendid that he could think of nothing
else all day, he retired to the forest to conduct his scientific experiment in fasting.

Anguished by the hunger burning in his vitals, he began to hallucinate and saw his forefathers, who appeared threateningly before him. He held them responsible for his life of misery, but he dared not say so openly. He says, "it was they who involved our dog life in guilt, and so I could easily have responded to their menaces with countermenaces; but I bow before their knowledge, it comes from sources which we know no longer, and for that reason, much as I may feel compelled to oppose them, I shall never actually overstep their laws, but content myself with wriggling out through the gaps, for which I have a particularly good nose" (GW, 66).

In order to conduct his fasting experiment, the dog had separated himself from his fellows by an infinite distance so that no one could possibly come to his aid even if he were dying. The young dog was willing to risk his life "to achieve truth and escape from this world of falsehood" (GW, 70). After undergoing endless torment, he fainted from hunger. When he recovered, he found himself lying in a pool of blood that he had vomited. A strange dog stood before him who told him to leave, but he was so feeble that he answered that he couldn't leave even if he wanted to. The beautiful hunter dog told him that he could go away slowly despite his feebleness, for if he remained, he would race off later on. At any other time, the investigating dog would have been delighted to submit to "the blandishments of such a beautiful creature," but at that moment, the thought filled him with terror, and he screamed, "Get out!"

The hunter dog started to retreat reluctantly, saying: "You're wonderful. Don't I please you?" The investigating dog suddenly began to realize that something remarkable was about to happen. He began to plead with the hunter hound to forget his hunting and remain with him, but the hunter insisted that he could not do this while the investigating dog lay there. After some discussion, the narrating dog noticed that the hound was "preparing to upraise" a song. A miracle was happening: the hunter dog was singing without knowing it and the melody was floating in the air, moving toward him. A "sort of grandeur" illumined the dog which was the "sole, even if delusive, reality" which he carried over to the world after his great fast.

The investigating dog, who was exalted and transfigured by this apotheosis has never been able to annihilate or forget this experience. He was actually beside himself. The music which emanated from the hunter dog seemed to exist only for his sake, "this voice before whose sublimity the woods fell silent" seemed to exist only for him. The dog had at last met another dog that could nourish him, whose music existed only for him and to whom he responded with his whole being.

The investigating dog never experienced this apotheosis again. Obliged to keep the silence, he never mentioned this encounter to any of his friends. Since this experience the investigating dog has become absorbed in more profound researches. He is now investigating the border region between the science of food and the science of music. He had risked his life to "achieve truth and escape from a world of falsehood"; instead he miraculously achieved a moment of ecstasy.

The dog now prizes freedom above anything else on earth. Freedom will give him the time and energy to concentrate on his investigations and he will steep himself in the problems of those who are forced to lead a dog's life in his culture. He will nourish himself on his researches and he will have freedom. The freedom he will possess is indeed a wretched business, "But nevertheless freedom, nevertheless a possession" (GW, 78).

4

The Judgment

Franz Kafka had not thought seriously about marriage until he was about twenty-five years old. He wrote his father that although he had shown prescience in his choice of a career, "I showed no foresight at all with regard to the significance and possibility of a marriage" (DF, 181). This, "the greatest terror" of his life, confronted him "almost completely unexpectedly" when he began to make the first of his "large-scale and hopeful" attempts to escape from his father's orbit by getting married. Up to that time, he had had no inkling that "a permanent, decisive, and indeed . . . grimly bitter ordeal was imminent" (DF, 181–82).

He had had "a certain temporary mistrust of his sexual capacity in his youth" (B, 37), but his doubts about his virility were of a short duration; he had had several experiences with prostitutes which had reassured him on that score. He found these experiences obscene and horrible (M, 163); but, in 1909, his yearning to join the circle of humanity had become so pervasive that he thought it might be possible for him to split off his homosexual self, and, like his hero, Raban (kavka), he fantasied himself leaving his true self at home in bed in the form of a beetle while the outer shell of his clothed body would go through the motions of making wedding preparations (DF, 6).

Marriage, for Kafka, had come to represent a panacea for all of his problems. He tried to convince himself that if he could "pass the test of marriage in spite of everything," he might be able to "steer it in a direction favorable" to his "development" (DI, 297). But Kafka was a realist and knew this hope was absurd; it was only when he was at the brink of suicide that he grasped at this belief.

Nevertheless, Kafka hoped against hope that marriage might cure him of his wound. Only by marrying would he be able to become a man like his father; only by marrying would he become his father's equal. Marriage would make him free and guiltless; his father would become untyrannical and sympathetic. But marriage was barred to him because it was "precisely and particularly" his father's "most intimate domain" (DF, 190–91). In his letter to his father, Kafka described to him what constituted this domain: "Sometimes I imagine a map of the world spread out flat and you stretched out diagonally across it. And what I feel then is that only those territories come into question for my life that either are not covered by you or are not within your reach. And in keeping with the conception that I have of your magnitude, these are not many and not very comforting territories, and above all marriage is not among them" (DF, 191).

Ten years after he wrote "The Judgment," Kafka assumed the role of K., a land surveyor, and set out to measure the boundaries of *The Castle*, which represented his Father's domain. The Castle authorities refused to permit him to practice his profession. His inexorable attempts to find a place where he could exist in his own image were fruitless. The castle had no need of a land-surveyor. Its frontiers had all been "marked out and officially recorded" (C, 77). In a diary entry written at about the time he was writing *The Castle*, Kafka asked: "why did I want to quit the world? Because 'he' [his father] would not let me live in it, in his world" (DII, 213).

Max Brod mentioned that Kafka, like Joseph K. of *The Trial*, was greedy for life and snatched "at the world with twenty hands" (T, 282). He felt a desperate need for personal happiness, and despite his homosexual orientation, he yearned to have a wife and children and to experience the joy of living like other men. Therefore, when he was twenty-nine years old, he made a firm decision to get married. Since women, for him, were merely representatives who would open the door to the normal life he wished to lead, he permitted himself to be governed by chance (DF, 188) in his choice of a mate. He decided to make a marriage of common sense (DF, 189) and to choose a girl who would be appropriate.

Six weeks before he wrote "The Judgment," Kafka met Felice Bauer in Max Brod's parents' house, and came to an unshakable opinion. He had finally found a girl who met his specifications. He described this meeting in a diary entry on August 20, 1912: "Miss F. B. When I arrived at Brod's on August 13th, she was sitting at the table. I was not at all curious about who she was, but rather took her for granted at once. Bony, empty face that wore its emptiness openly. Bare throat. A blouse thrown on. Looked very domestic in her dress, although, as it later turned out, she by no means was. . . . Almost broken nose. Blond, somewhat straight, unattractive hair, strong chin. As I was taking my seat, I looked at her closely for the first time, by the time I was seated I already had an unshakable opinion." Obviously his "unshakable opinion" was not based on the fascination of the moth for the flame.

Despite his resolute determination, Kafka immediately became tormented with anxiety and indecision. It was merely his outer self that had come to his unshakable opinion. The seismograph of his heart, which had been registering an earthquake going on within him since he made his decision, made him acutely aware that there were two dissenting aspects of himself which were violately opposed to his decision: his inner depth, which was his euphemism for his homosexual inner self; and his irrational, dictatorial conscience.

In order to deal with the insurmountable problems

arising from his resolution to get married, Kafka, who thought in images, painted a psychological triptych in which he depicted himself as three different characters and described the dynamic interplay of these three warring aspects of his personality. Georg was his outer image or ego; his Russian friend played the role of his unconscious, which Kafka believed was the source of his homosexuality and the fountainhead of his genius and creativity; and Mr. Bendemann, who was modeled on Kafka's childish image of his father—an inconsistent, unpredictable, irrational figure, which had terrified Kafka throughout his lifetime, represented his conscience or his superego. In her brilliant interpretation of "The Judgment," Kate Flores mentioned that Kafka clothed his inner-self in a business suit and set him to work in a warehouse in Russia where he was engaged in the "trade" of writing. Kafka's pathological superego, Mr. Bendemann, was clad in a dirty, shabby bathrobe and resided in an airless cluttered cell in one of the compartments of Kafka's mind. Kafka identified his chief protagonists in a diary entry (DI, 278–79). The Bendemann family were the Kafkas and Fräulein Brandenfeld was Felice Bauer, Kafka's prospective fiancée. He made a point of mentioning that Georg (who was indistinguishable from himself) "believed he had his father within him," indicating that Mr. Bendemann was not Hermann Kafka; rather he was the image of the father which Kafka had incorporated within himself. He was therefore an incorporeal figure and existed only in the recesses of Georg's/Kafka's mind.

Kafka did not clearly identify the Russian friend, but most critics today concede that he is either the image of Kafka, the writer, or his alter ego. That he was Kafka, the writer, was implicit symbolically in his description: he was the facsimile of all of Kafka's writer-images and looked as if he were made of yellow paper. Kate Flores pointed out that his tattered wares were his manuscripts and discarded papers, his showcases displayed his finished literary creations and his gas fixtures provided light for his nighttime writing, which he did in cooperation with Kafka. The Russian friend provided the subject matter and the inspiration and Kafka provided the pen.

The Russian friend was a mirror reflection of the investigating dog. He had removed himself from the general life of the community (PC, 49–50) and of "his fellow countrymen out there and had almost no social intercourse with Russian families" (PC, 49–50). Like the bachelor in "Moment of Torment," he could live only as a hermit; like the kavka-dog, he was "wearing himself out to no purpose" (PC, 49), ceaselessly occupied in writing his philosophical reflections and incredible stories. Kafka also identified the Russian friend symbolically by the use of his code. Like all of Kafka's homosexual protagonists, the Russian friend was afflicted with an inner imperfection: "his skin was growing so yellow as to indicate some latent disease" (PC, 49). Since in all of Kafka's works the term *latent disease* is used to symbolize homosexual orientation, it becomes obvious why the Russian friend had determined to remain "a permanent bachelor" (PC, 50).

The Russian friend lived in Russia symbolically; literally, however, he lived within the depth of Georg/ Kafka. Kafka believed that his inner depth was the seat of his true identity which he had been forced to conceal from the world. He tried to suppress and split off his homosexual self so that it had become disembodied and was living a life of its own, hidden deep in the wastes of himself, so far away that it might just as well have been in Russia. We mentioned that, in Kafka's writings, Russia and the north of China represent those vast, icy wastelands which provide a haven for Kafka's sexual deviants. These men are rebels of necessity because the authorities of their culture consider them outside the law. Kafka's heroes refuse to recognize the law that makes them pariahs and calls them criminals; they have a law of their own to which they adhere. In the episode in which the Russian friend tells the "incredible" story of the priest who cuts a cross on the palm of his hand

and holds it up to quiet the raging mob, the Russian friend was unquestionably one of the rioters. Kafka, by his own admission, had very little faith in Jewish tradition at the time he was writing this story; he had no faith at all in Christianity. In 1914, when Brod tried desperately to get him involved in religion and in the Jewish problem, Kafka became so angry that he almost broke up the relationship. He wrote in his diary on January 1914: "What have I in common with Jews? I have hardly anything in common with myself" (DII, 11). Kafka reinforced his identification of the Russian friend as a homosexual by stating that he had "run off the rails" (PC, 50). In the language of Kafka's concrete metaphors, this indicated that he had lost his direction in life because the needle of his sexual aims had become polarized in an opposite direction and he could no longer pursue the path other men followed in their search for sexual gratification.

The first panel of the triptych was painted in the style of Picasso and presented two faces of Georg/Kafka merging into each other. The first image represented the impression Kafka believed he made on his acquaintances and most of his intimate friends. It depicted a smug, complacent extrovert; a dilettante in writing, the charming son of a rich, bourgeois father whom he regarded with thinly veiled scorn and hostility. The second image indicated what Kafka thought of himself. It was the portrait of an extremely timid young man who wore a mask of self-assurance and indifference, beneath which was a terrified child inordinately ambivalent in the violence of his love and hatred for his father. Since Kafka was a consummate artist, neither of the portraits in the first panel was a photographic likeness. Certain elements of his personality emerged of which he may not have been fully aware. Kafka could not have realized the significance of his withering description of Felice Bauer in his diary notes. Georg mirrors Kafka in his description of his fiancée. He has nothing to say about Fräulein Brandenfeld except that she is well-to-do, but this seems so impressive that it warrants Georg's mentioning it twice.

The portrait of Georg also inadvertently disclosed Kafka's conflict between his philistine, bourgeois standards and his bohemian, artistic values. Kafka had always known that he could not compete with his father in a struggle for financial supremacy, but that did not deter him from eating sour grapes. Kafka always spoke warmly and admiringly of his father's business success and the rewards that the community had heaped upon him, but he was a bit envious of his father's achievements. Despite this envy, Kafka never made any serious attempt to achieve a spectacular business success. He could not waste his time and energy striving for bourgeois values.

In all of his narratives, Kafka is ironic and is telling the opposite of the truth when he writes about the financial success of his heroes, all of whom are indistinguishable from himself. In "The Judgment," when Georg hypocritically refuses to ascribe his phenomenal business success to his own efforts yet patently reveals that he alone is responsible for the enormous upsurge in business (PC, 51), Kafka is being ironic and is evading the truth. Georg's success is like the magical thinking in dreams in which a person does not have to struggle to become a millionaire: he is one. It is necessary to discount Georg's success. Georg shared Kafka's financial problems which played an important part in his marriage plans.

As a matter of fact, Georg/Kafka had briefly considered recalling his writer-image from Russia. This signified symbolically that he was thinking of giving up his writing career. Kafka knew that he could not support a family on the proceeds of his writings. His position in the Workers' Accident Insurance Institute provided him with an adequate living for himself, but he lived with his family and his needs were minimal. Even this relatively nontaxing position, which occupied six hours of his day, was excessively irksome because it drained him of the energy he needed for his creative writing. He knew intuitively that Felice Bauer would want "the average: a comfortable home, an interest in my part in the factory, good food, bed at eleven, central heating" (DII, 111). It would become necessary for him to supplement his income by working afternoons at the factory in which he had an interest with his father, and he would then have no time or energy left for his writing, which was his sole gratification in life and his only justification for living.

During the three years preceding the writing of "The Judgment" Kafka had fallen into a literary morass and had been unable to write anything of note. He had had an initial success, reflected in the Russian friend's flourishing business, but since then, his writing, like his Russian friend's business, "had long been going downhill" (PC, 49). He considered himself a failure and thought of giving up writing, but he dismissed this idea as rapidly as did Georg when he thought of recalling his Russian friend. Kate Flores identified the three letters Georg sent to his Russian friend as images of Kafka's literary creations. We suggest that they may have been "Description of a Struggle," "Wedding Preparations in the Country," and "Meditations." These works deal symbolically with the plight of a homosexual bachelor and his consuming need to join the circle of humanity by getting married.

Kafka had been delving into his unconscious for many years in order to obtain a deeper understanding of himself and had arrived at valuable psychological insights. He had carefully studied Freud's works while attending discussion groups and lecture series at the home of Bertha Fanta, who invited such members of the intellectually elite as Albert Einstein to lecture to her study groups. Many psychologists today hold Kafka in high esteem. Eric Fromm, for example, gives credit to Freud, Aristotle, Spinoza, and Kafka for contributing to his understanding of psychology. Just as Shakespeare, Goethe, Dostoevski, Mann, and Proust seemed to have an intuitive grasp of unconscious processes, so Kafka was able to understand instinctively what the great psychologists of his day were saying in psychodynamic terms and was able to translate these insights into the portrayal of his characters.

It is probable that Kafka anticipated some of Freud's major discoveries. The tribal father that Kafka depicts in "The Judgment" was described at just the time Freud published *Totem and Taboo*. Kafka may have written "The Judgment" before he had read this book. He certainly had the psychological insight to visualize the tribal chief of Freud's description. In 1912, the "unconscious" was as loosely defined by most psychologists as it is confusedly defined today. That did not deter Kafka from dissecting himself into three parts and delineating his outer image, loosely defined as his ego, as Georg; his inner depth, which he called his unconscious, as the Russian friend; and his tyrannical conscience or superego as Mr. Bendemann. Kafka, who was no slavish adherent of any school of psychology, evolved his own theories of the dynamics of personality.

Simply by refraining from using psychological nomenclature and personifying his unconscious and his tyrannical superego so that they appeared as corporeal and substantial as if they were people, Kafka created the miracle of this plot. He had mentioned in his diary (DI, 276) that he had thoughts of Freud while writing this story, but none of his exegetes realized that this narrative was a graphic expression of Freud's theories of the functioning of the unconscious. The Russian friend, who was the most important and active protagonist in this tale was, of course, present throughout this nightmarish narrative. He was invisible, but he motivated and manipulated Georg in "peculiar ways" from the beginning to the end of the story.

When Kafka sat down to write this tale, he was immediately confronted by his Russian friend, who represented his unconscious (very loosely defined). It was the Russian friend who dictated the story; Kafka was merely his amanuensis. Kafka gave his Russian friend full credit for this tale in his diary notes, stating: "The story came out of me like a real birth, covered with filth and slime, and only I have the hand that can reach to the body itself and the strength and desire to do so" (DI, 278). Kafka knew "The Judgment" was a revelatory nightmare and that he was the only one who could interpret it correctly. He tried at first to heed the warning of his unconscious, and three months after he had met F. B., he attempted to put an end to the relationship. He wrote F. B. a letter telling her that the correspondence between them must stop. He was "past all help," and if he persisted in clinging to her, he deserved "to be cursed" (B, 140). Nevertheless, the correspondence continued. At times Felice became very uneasy with her suitor who waxed when she waned and became fearful and withdrawn when she responded.

One year after the first anniversary of their meeting, Kafka finally decided to put an end to the affair. He wrote in his diary that what each would suffer by ending their relationship would be nothing to compare "with the common suffering that would result" if they continued to torment each other (DI, 295). The next day he received three letters from F. B., which he could not resist. He made a diary entry saying: "I love her as far as I am capable of it, but the love lies buried to the point of suffocation under fear and self-reproaches." On that day, he proposed to Felice Bauer and wrote in his diary: "Conclusion for my case from 'The Judgment.' . . . Georg goes to pieces because of his fiancée" (DI, 296).

On the morning following his proposal, Kafka was suicidal and thought of jumping through the window (DI, 296). When the official engagement ceremony took place in Berlin in June 1914, he felt "bound like a criminal" (B, 145). The physical aspects of marriage terrified him and he wrote: "Coitus as punishment for the happiness of being together. Live as ascetically as possible, more ascetically than a bachelor, that is the only possible way for me to endure marriage. But she?" (DI, 296). He had confided to Max Brod: "The very idea of a honeymoon fills me with horror" (B, 144). The engagement wreaked havoc with his already precarious mental balance, and, like Georg in "The Judgment," he began to "go to pieces." Two months after the engagement ceremony, he met with Felice Bauer and her family in Berlin to terminate the engagement. He called the hotel in which they met a "court of law," a "Tribunal in a hotel" (DII, 65) foreshadowing the imagery of *The Trial*. At that time he echoed the indictment of his tyrannical superego in "The Judgment" characterizing himself as "devilish in my innocence."

Kafka had carefully studied Freud's *Psychopathology of Everyday Life* (E, 513) at Bertha Fanta's discussion group and agreed with Freud that unconscious motivations determine conscious behavior. Kafka believed, as Freud did, that if he said or did anything in contradiction to his unconscious wishes, his unconscious would cause him to make a slip, to blunder, to forget what he wanted to do or say, or to trip and have an accident. Kafka gave the reader a number of clues to the fact that "The Judgment" was a psychological exercise in the dynamics of the forces working within him by demonstrating that his unconscious, the Russian friend, acted in accordance with Freud's theories. When Georg told his fiancée that he had decided not to send an engagement announcement to his Russian friend because he had no intention of inviting him to his wedding, his fiancée, who was as intuitive as she was well-to-do, became quite alarmed. She had heard a great deal about the Russian friend, and the more she heard the more disturbed she became. She sensed that she was being courted by a man who outwardly desired to marry her but inwardly was violently opposed to the marriage. She insisted that Georg invite his friend to the wedding because she did not want to marry a man who was divided against himself. When Georg disagreed, explaining that he did not want to hurt his friend's feelings, she became angry and exclaimed: "Since your friends are like that, Georg, you shouldn't ever have got engaged at all." Georg tried to

reassure her, but his unconscious, his Russian friend and
inseparable companion, intervened and caused him to
make a slip. Instead of saying what he wanted to say,
Georg mouthed the words of his invisible friend and
remarked: "Well, we're both to blame for that," then
realizing that he was reproaching his fiancée as well as
himself for the mistake they had made in getting engaged, Georg immediately said: "but I wouldn't have it
any other way now," reinforcing his reassurance with
kisses. Fräulein Brandenfeld responded fervently to
Georg's kisses, but her apprehension remained unabated
and she said, "All the same, I do feel upset."

Georg was now in a quandary. Since he wanted at the
same time and with the same intensity to marry and not
to marry, he could not ignore his fiancée's anxiety. If
she became too apprehensive, she might break the engagement. It was then that Georg steeled himself to confess to his Russian friend that he had become engaged
to Fräulein Frieda Brandenfeld, a girl from a well-
to-do family (PC, 52). So reluctant was Georg to confess his engagement that, although he had stated previously that he had nothing to say to his friend, he wrote
a very long letter leaving this succulent tidbit to the very
end. Georg then proceeded to suggest that there were
excellent reasons why his friend should not come to the
wedding and ended with: "do just as seems good to you
without regarding any interests but your own." Georg
did not want his Russian friend to come to his wedding.
He was afraid he might cause him to trip on the way to
the altar and have a very serious accident.

In reporting this incident, Kafka was demonstrating
one of the ways in which Georg/Kafka was manipulated
by his unconscious as well as one of the "peculiar ways"
in which his unconscious, which could not communicate with him directly, tried to communicate with him.
Georg's/Kafka's unconscious was trying to tell him in
its own peculiar fashion (PC, 52) that his engagement
was a terrible mistake and that he must break it immediately. However Georg was so intent on reassuring

his fiancée after he had made the dreadful slip that he had no time to listen to his Russian friend's excellent advice.

The Russian friend behaved according to Freud's theories of the functioning of the unconscious with some interesting Kafkan variations. He demanded gratification for his sexual needs. That they were deviant did not concern the Russian friend at all. When Georg/Kafka refused to acquiesce to his Russian friend's demands for sexual gratification, the Russian rebel within Georg declared war or started a revolution. The political situation in Russia became "uncertain" (PC, 51), and Kafka/Georg experienced the symptoms of inner conflict. When the political situation in Russia became explosive, Kafka suffered from bodily symptoms and mental anguish.

Kafka believed that his unconscious was the most powerful component of his personality and demonstrated this belief in "The Judgment" by indicating that Georg (the ego) was the most pusillanimous aspect of his self. The father-image or superego conclusively showed that he was superior to Georg by making mincemeat of him. The father-image, however, was the inferior of the Russian friend by definition: he was the subordinate of the Russian friend because he was his representative.

At about 1900, hypnosis was very widely used by Freud and other psychiatrists and was a favored form of therapy. By 1912, Freud no longer used hypnosis, but it was still widely used by other psychiatrists. From the structure of this story, one gathers that when Kafka wrote "The Judgment," in 1912, he seems to have evolved the interesting theory that his unconscious could exert a hypnotic influence over him. It could absent his mind; then it would suggest that he obey its instructions. At such times, Kafka was under the spell of forces beyond his control. Kafka would then behave as though he were acting in a dream for which his unconscious had written the script.

In "The Judgment," Georg was in a dreamlike state throughout the entire story. In the first paragraph, Kafka had mentioned that Georg put the letter in an envelope in a "dreamy fashion." After he had finished the letter, he "barely acknowledged, with an absent smile, a greeting waved to him from the street by a passing acquaintance" because his mind was absent. That Georg's mind had been vacated before he entered Mr. Bendemann's room was manifested by the fact that he "vacantly" followed the old man's movements (PC, 55). At the end of the story, Georg felt "urged" from the bedroom by his Russian friend's hypnotic suggestion and rushed madly to the bridge to execute the sentence (PC, 63). During the entire time Georg was in the father-image's room, he was under the hypnotic control of his Russian friend who had vacated his mind so that Georg would do his bidding. That is why Georg kept forgetting everything he wanted to do or say; that is why he stuttered and blundered and bungled and crouched into corners. Everything he did and said worked against him. He had regressed to the stage of a terrified little boy who was being filled with intolerable guilt by his father. He could not wait to execute his father-image's verdict because he felt that only by being punished could he regain the love and forgiveness of his father.

The portrait of Mr. Bendemann, which appeared in the third panel of the triptych, is simultaneously Mr. Hermann Kafka *and* the father-image upon which Franz Kafka had become fixated in early childhood. This portrait is probably one of Kafka's most dramatic literary achievements. Kafka seems to have deliberately created this confusing image to indicate that he himself could not differentiate between these two figures. Kafka was aware of his father-fixation as well as of his inability to cure himself of it. Realistically, he saw his father as he was: a smug, successful, middle-class businessman, inconsistent and intolerant, a ham actor, a frustrated old man who had futilely tried to suppress his son's individuality not because he was malicious but because he could recognize no values other than his own.

Kafka never made any attempt to equal or surpass his

father in any of the areas which his father deemed important. He knew better than to engage in a struggle for economic supremacy. However, Kafka did engage in a lifelong struggle with his father to maintain his own individuality. Despite his crippling love for his father, he never permitted him to obliterate his identity, even though he felt stricken with guilt whenever he engaged in independent action of any kind. Like Mr. Bendemann, Hermann Kafka disapproved of every activity in which his son was interested; even reading had been a bone of contention between father and son. Kafka consistently circumvented his father's unreasonable demands and did exactly what he wanted to do; however his guilt increased as he continued to assert his individuality. In his letter to his father, Kafka stated: "I had lost my self-confidence where you were concerned, and in its place had developed a boundless sense of guilt. (In recollection of this boundlessness, I once wrote of someone, accurately: 'He is afraid the shame will outlive him even.')" (DF, 170). In *The Trial*, just as the knife is thrust into Joseph K.'s heart, he exclaims: "Like a dog, . . . it was as if the shame of it must outlive him" (T, 286). (The reader will note that in his letter to his father, Kafka confuses guilt with shame.)

Kafka's unholy alliance with his father was patent to his intimate friends. Max Brod knew even before he had seen Kafka's diary that Kafka's "deepest wound . . . was just this—how he overestimated his father" and longed for his approval (B, 23). Brod described Kafka as a man haunted by a father-image and wrote of Kafka's futile attempts to escape from his father's orbit. He stated that Kafka's pathological involvement with his father "lasted to the end of his life as 'a general load of fear, weakness, and self contempt'" (B, 23). In "The Judgment," Kafka describes the pathological father-image which had become a part of himself and which distorted Kafka's view of all fathers and all authority figures. His father's voice was never the "voice of one single father" (PC, 87). It was the hissing, shouting, and screaming of all the tyrannical authority figures in the universe.

In his conception of the sadistic, rampaging father-image, Kafka displayed his psychological as well as his literary genius. For the first time in the history of psychology, Kafka described in graphic form the pathological superego which exists in certain mentally ill individuals and in some types of criminal personalities. When Kafka assigned Mr. Bendemann to play the role of the "representative" of his Russian friend (the id—*very* loosely defined), he used the same terminology and described the same dynamic concept Freud used more than a decade later in his description of the superego as the representative of the id. Adherents of Freud's psychoanalytic school will probably quarrel with Kafka's definitions of his concepts, but it must be remembered that Freud had not yet clearly defined any of these terms.

In *The Ego and the Id*, which was published in 1923, Freud explained that there is a pathological type of superego which forms an unholy alliance with the id for the purpose of destroying the ego. This superego rages against the ego, filling it with boundless, unconscious guilt. It compels certain types of criminal personalities to commit a crime merely for the purpose of being punished so that they can gain relief from their unconscious guilt. These criminals commit crimes so carelessly and obviously that they are bound to be apprehended and punished. This is the only way in which they can be relieved of their boundless guilt. This pathological superego also appears in certain depressed individuals who are filled with a sense of overwhelming guilt. It urges these individuals to commit suicide, which is the most drastic kind of self-punishment. In the portrait of Mr. Bendemann, Kafka portrayed for the first time in psychological history the dynamics of this pathological superego.

We mentioned that Kafka identified Mr. Bendemann as his father-image in his diary notes, stating: "Georg believes he has his father within him," but Kafka had not been niggardly in providing the reader with clues to

indicate that the Mr. Bendemann in the airtight cell
was not Mr. Hermann Kafka. In all of Kafka's writings
dark, dingy, airtight, and hot rooms are symbols for the
compartments of his mind. Many of these rooms appear in *The Trial*. Dirty family linens are washed in
these rooms in the figurative sense of the term. The
dirty underwear that Mr. Bendemann was wearing,
which Georg had resolved to have washed, was symbolic
of the family conflict in this story. In this airtight room,
Mr. Bendemann appeared like a "giant of a man"; Georg
had mentioned that "in business hours he's quite different" (PC, 55), implying that Hermann Kafka was
certainly not a Jehovah-like figure; he was a toothless,
emaciated, feeble old man in the world of reality, except
in his son's eyes. In all of Kafka's tales, the bachelor son
occupies the least desirable room in the house. Merely
by placing Mr. Bendemann in a dark, dingy, cluttered,
and airless room, which he would never have chosen if
there were a bright, sunny room available, Kafka gave a
clue that the occupant of this room could not have been
Hermann Kafka. Moreover, Kafka gave the reader a final
clue by mentioning that Mr. Bendemann had a scar,
which was his symbol for homosexuality. Mr. Hermann
Kafka was certainly not a homosexual.

The confusing elements of this story stem from the
fact that Kafka's pathological superego, which had been
modeled on the image he had had of his father in childhood, had become the facsimile of Mr. Hermann Kafka's
volatile, ill-tempered, dictatorial personality, magnified
to gigantic proportions. When Mr. Bendemann, Kafka's
superego, began to rant and rave, Georg acted exactly as
Kafka had behaved when his father engaged in his ti-
rades. He became mindless and speechless; he was almost distracted and tried to shrink into the nearest
corner.

Kafka had refrained from using psychological terminology in this story and did not reveal overtly that Mr.
Bendemann was Georg's/Kafka's conscience, but he described his behavior in such a way that it became evident

that he played the role of Kafka's pathological super-ego. From the beginning to the end of his explosive out-burst he accused Georg of every perfidy and filled him with boundless guilt. This was no quarrel between a father and a son; it was an abusive diatribe delivered by a tyrannical, inconsistent, and unrealistic pathological conscience. That Mr. Bendemann represented Kafka's pathological superego was incontrovertibly proved when Kafka broke his first engagement to F. B. in 1914, two months after the engagement ceremony. At that time, Kafka characterized himself as "devilish in my inno-cence" (DII, 65) repeating almost the identical words of accusation made by Mr. Bendemann in "The Judg-ment." It was Kafka's conscience which accused him of every misdeed; Franz Kafka himself rendered the verdict and pronounced his own sentence: "Death by drown-ing."

When Kafka wrote "The Judgment," he felt for the first time that he had discovered a structure which would conceal his identity completely yet permit him to con-fess the whole truth about himself. Since the story ap-peared in the form of a nightmare, the truth would be incomprehensible to his readers. He had created a me-dium in which the truth could be told; it would then be destroyed as if by fire; but in the very act of destruc-tion, a resurrection would take place and the truth would appear as a lie. Kafka wrote exultantly of his great dis-covery: "How everything can be said, how for every-thing, for the strangest fancies, there waits a great fire in which they perish and rise up again" (DI, 276). "The Judgment" was the first story which Kafka willingly gave to Brod for publication. He considered it to be the great-est of his literary achievements and read it frequently to his friends. Max Brod reports that when Kafka read the story at Oskar Baum's, shortly after he had written it, he had tears in his eyes and said: "The indubitability of the story is confirmed." Max Brod observed: "These are strong words of self-conviction, rare enough in the case of Kafka" (B, 141).

The reasons Georg had given for not visiting Mr. Bendemann in his cell-like room were sheer rationalizations. Georg would never have ventured into his father-image's room if he had been in full possession of his wits. He had wandered mindlessly into the bedroom, like a person following a posthypnotic suggestion. His Russian friend had vacated his mind and propelled him into Mr. Bendemann's room because he had found it impossible to go on living. Georg had persisted in denying him every gratification because of his tyrannical conscience. The Russian friend had felt betrayed by Georg's engagement. He knew that Georg/Kafka would not be able to endure living with a woman. If Georg were to marry, the Russian friend knew he would live more ascetically (DI, 296) than he had been living as a bachelor. For years the Russian friend had been starving for sexual gratification and he was going to pieces. He decided that he would prefer to drown rather than to die of slow starvation. Since he had not the power to commit suicide and since he could not communicate with Georg directly, he made an alliance with Mr. Bendemann for the purpose of getting Georg to destroy himself.

The Russian friend knew that if he could get Georg to confront his tyrannical superego, Mr. Bendemann, he would see to it that Georg would be filled with boundless guilt. Since Georg's only desire was to get the love and approval of his father-image, he would want Mr. Bendemann to punish him for his terrible crimes. Only by being punished would he be able to relieve himself of his intolerable guilt. Mr. Bendemann would convince Georg that he was such a reprobate that there was no reason why he should go on living. Then he would sentence him to death. As soon as Mr. Bendemann would pronounce the sentence, the Russian friend would take over and urge (PC, 63) Georg to rush from the room to the bridge where he would put an end to his Russian friend's misery as well as his own. As for Mr. Bendemann, he would topple from the bed and smash himself.

The trinity of the father, the son, and the Russian friend would all expire at the same moment. This is the dynamic description of the workings of the pathological superego graphically described in somewhat simplistic terms.

It is necessary to point out that the Russian friend was not to blame for appointing Mr. Bendemann as his representative. He had needed a representative in order to communicate directly with Georg. The unconscious cannot communicate directly with the ego. It therefore makes an alliance with the superego so that it can make its wants known directly to the ego. It works in this fashion: When the unconscious desires any kind of gratification, it sends a message to the conscience telling it exactly what it wants. If the conscience is healthy and realistic, it permits the unconscious to gratify itself if it can do so without danger to the ego. The healthy conscience does not fill the ego with guilt and fear unless the unconscious makes unrealistic, dangerous demands. It closes its eyes to minor transgressions. If Georg had had a gentle, tolerant, consistent, realistic father-image for his conscience, the Russian friend would have been delighted to deal with him. According to psychological principles, anyone who became Georg's superego would automatically become the Russian friend's representative.

When Georg entered Mr. Bendemann's bedroom, he saw his father-image reading an ancient newspaper, held to one side to correct a "defect of vision" (PC, 54). In the language of Kafka's concrete metaphors, this meant that the old man couldn't see what was in front of his nose. His vision was biased and slanted so that he could see only one side of an issue—his own. Since Mr. Bendemann had been imprisoned in this airtight chamber from the time Kafka had become fixated upon his father, the newspaper Mr. Bendemann was reading was approximately a quarter of a century old. That was why Georg could not recognize it. This newspaper was Mr. Bendemann's sole interest. He could not bear to be parted from it and carried it to his bed when his son lovingly deposited him there. It is probable that the newspaper may have contained various items indicating why Mr. Bendemann had been incarcerated in this cell. The mementoes of the mother that cluttered up the walls probably indicated the part she had played in contributing to her son's father-fixation, which later manifested itself in his latent disease. She had allied herself with her husband to whom she gave so much of her strength (PC, 61) that she had none left to give to her son.

The unpredictable Mr. Bendemann graciously arose to greet his son as if he were welcoming an honored guest. He removed the soiled dishes with the remnants of his uneaten breakfast to a a chest in honor of his visitor. The newspaper which he was reading, held to one side, indicated as we explained that he was extremely biased and could see only one side of an issue; however, Georg's vision was equally defective. As the toothless, emaciated, disheveled old man came eagerly toward him, he saw only the father-image he had created in his mind and thought, "My father is still a giant of a man." (The confusion in this confrontation derives from Kafka's contrapuntal treatment of Mr. Bendemann as father-image or his superego and his real father. The reader must constantly be alert to determine which of these figures is speaking.)

The invisible Russian friend, who was present at this scene, had noted the father-image's welcoming gestures and realized that he must see to it that Georg do or say something to provoke a quarrel. Georg's first remark aroused the enmity of his father-image. He said, "It's unbearably dark here." Mr. Bendemann, who had been serving time in this dark cell for about a quarter of a century, responded bleakly, "Yes, it's dark enough." Mr. Bendemann would never have chosen this room of his own accord. Georg continued to blunder, saying, "And you've shut the window, too?" Mr. Bendemann's annoyance increased. He knew that the window was stuck fast and could never be opened. Since he was not in a mood to quarrel, and since he was a practical man, he brushed off his son's remark and said, "I prefer it like that."

Georg then announced that he was sending his thirty-day-old "news" of his engagement to his friend in St. Petersburg. The father-image became confused. His defect in vision had always prevented him from seeing both sides of his son. Confronted with his living son, he momentarily forgot about his invisible homosexual son, who resided in the vast wastes of Russia, secreted in the inner depths of his living son. He asked: "To St. Petersburg?" Georg explained: "To my friend there."

Mr. Bendemann, who was very sharp, noticed that his son became embarrassed and could not meet his eye (PC, 55). At that moment, Georg was viewing his father-image with awe, thinking, "How solidly he sits here with his arms crossed," but Mr. Bendemann misinterpreted his son's embarrassment. He suddenly realized that Georg was referring to his invisible self, the Russian friend who had always been a source of acute embarrassment to both of them. Now Mr. Bendemann said "with peculiar emphasis" (PC, 55), "Oh yes. To your friend." Georg, who was being manipulated by his Russian friend and could not refrain from bungling, explained that he had not sent his friend an engagement announcement and wasn't ever going to send one. Mr. Bendemann sat quietly, giving his son enough rope; he had not yet decided whether or not he wanted to quarrel. He asked: "And now, you've changed your mind?"

When his son had the effrontery to say: "I said to myself, my being happily engaged should make him happy too," the father-image began to bristle. Since he was Georg's/Kafka's conscience, he knew the whole story. He knew that the Russian friend was a homosexual who would not be at all happy if he were presented with a wife. Mr. Bendemann showed his displeasure by lengthening his toothless mouth and saying: "You've come to me about this business, to talk it over with me. . . . But it's nothing; it's worse than nothing, if you

don't tell me the whole truth." We mentioned that one
of Kafka's major motifs is the passionate, almost frantic
need of his characters to hear the whole truth; it is as if
they are convinced that the whole truth can never be
revealed.

The Russian friend had judged Mr. Bendemann correctly. He had realized that he could not rely upon him
to start an argument. Mr. Bendemann had become very
old and feeble. He was not equal to things any longer;
his memory was failing. His wife's death had hit him
very hard. He would have preferred to avoid a conflict
and gave his son a chance to tell the whole truth. He
therefore pleaded, "I beg you, Georg, don't deceive me.
It's a trivial affair, it's hardly worth mentioning, so don't
deceive me. Do you really have this friend in St. Petersburg?" By the time Mr. Bendemann asked this question,
he knew that his son's answer would be a trivial matter
because Mr. Bendemann knew that Georg no longer
had a friend in St. Petersburg. Georg had betrayed his
friend by getting engaged.

We mentioned in our analysis of "Investigations of a
Dog" that, whenever Kafka structures a narrative in
which his characters represent various facets of his divided self, the various aspects of his self are alien to each
other, incomprehensible to each other, and at cross-
purposes with each other. Georg and his father had always been at cross-purposes. Therefore Georg misinterpreted his father-image's question. He knew Mr. Bendemann had known his inner self for about twenty-five
years and he could not understand why he did not
realize that Georg was discussing his invisible homosexual self. Georg suddenly thought that his father had
become senile. He loved his father and felt wretched
at his condition; yet simultaneously he felt an upsurge
of elation, emanating from his inner depths.

Now that his father had become senile, he could freely
express his deep love for his father which he had hitherto
buried within his innermost depths. Now that his mother
was dead, he would take care of his father. He would

take his mother's place. He would call a doctor and see to it that his father would follow the doctor's orders. He "made a quick, firm decision to take him into his own future establishment" (PC, 58). Georg had not given a thought to what would happen to his feeble old father before this interview; now he suddenly decided that he would never leave his father until death did them part. He could no longer refrain from expressing his overpowering love for his father and exclaimed: "A thousand friends wouldn't make up to me for my father."

Kafka had never been able to outgrow his inordinate love for his father because he had buried it within his innermost depths. We mentioned that Kafka believed that his homosexuality stemmed from the fact that his father had not only rejected every aspect of his individuality but had also rejected the love Franz had had for him since early childhood. Franz could not quench the love he had for his father; neither could he change himself into an image that his father might have accepted and loved. Deeply hurt at his father's rejection, Franz denied his love for his father and turned it into hostility. In his struggle to maintain his individuality, he leaned so far backward that he had become the anti-image of his father.

He had not been able to transfer his love to his mother because he felt that she was a confederate of his father. Hermann Kafka had never beaten Franz, but he would go through the preliminaries as if he were preparing for a hanging and Franz became more terrified than he would have been if he had gotten a whipping. Mrs. Kafka pleaded with her husband to spare Franz, just as Mrs. Samsa did in 'The Metamorphosis," but Franz always felt that his mother was allied with his father against him. The love which Franz had so deeply repressed could find no outlet and manifested itself in polymorphous-perverse infantile sexuality—narcissism, homosexuality, and incestuous desires.

In "The Judgment," Kafka revealed his incestuous feelings for his father in the scene in which he undressed him and lovingly put him to bed. Since "The Judgment" had come out of Kafka like a birth, it is possible that Kafka may have been completely unconscious of his incestuous love for his father. In "The Metamorphosis," Gregor openly displays his incestuous desire for his sister, which we shall discuss in our analysis of this story. It is possible that Kafka may have felt an overwhelming need to tell the whole truth and to reveal his love for his father in "The Judgment." He believed that in this story he had perfected a structure in which he could tell the whole truth with impunity.

In her interpretation of "The Judgment," Kate Flores comments:

> Kafka's hatred of his father has often been considered the cause of his sense of guilt; but of course a hatred as violent as Kafka's for his father is hardly to be distinguished from a love as violent. And hatred as a reaction to unattainability is not confined to abnormal cases of love; neither is the desire for the death of the beloved. Normally, however, these impulses are conscious, because socially acceptable, and may even be overtly expressed; whereas abnormally they are repressed when the love is unconscious, particularly when the love is unconscious, as it often is in the case of an Oedipus complex, the sufferer being aware chiefly of an intangible sense of guilt.

> May not this be the guilt Kafka dramatized in his writing, the agony, the self-contempt, the despair? From one point of view Kafka's life and work may be a long study in certain consequences upon the suppression of abnormal love; the ambivalent attitude of love and hate, the externalization of the inner struggle, the self-torturing conscientiousness and moral scrupulousness, the paralysis of the will, the dread of responsibility, the interminable rationalization tending to confuse issues in order to avoid decision, the fear, the hopelessness, the self-abasement, the masochism and sadism, the yearning for normalcy, the obsessive sense of guilt, and above all the delusions

of persecution. "I hate him because he persecutes me!" is the frequent cry of this sufferer, who longs unconsciously not only for the torture and death of his persecutor, but for torture and death at the hands of his beloved. (FKT, 21–22)

Drs. Calvin Hall and Richard Lind discovered in their analysis of Kafka's dreams that Kafka's Oedipus complex "is not inverted, nor is it normal; rather it is more like the female version of the Oedipus complex" (CHRL, 26); these authors characterized it as a "deviant Oedipal pattern" (CHRL, 70). This means that Kafka reacted to his father as if he were a female; he loved his father and wanted to assume his mother's role in relation to his father.

Kafka had endowed his father-image with a scar, which was always Kafka's symbol for homosexuality or deviant sexuality. Mr. Bendemann's scar was a battle wound which had completely healed. He had fought and won the battle to conquer his infantile sexuality; this had been evidenced in his happy marriage. But Kafka may have believed, as do some psychologists today, that this battle is never completely won. Now that Mr. Bendemann had regained the status of a bachelor due to the death of his wife, and had apparently become senile and childlike, Georg/Kafka may have wished, consciously or unconsciously, that the scar might reopen. (Mr. Hermann Kafka would not have had a scar. He escaped unscathed in his battle to attain maturity. Since Mr. Bendemann resided within the mind of Georg/Kafka, he shared his inner imperfection.)

Kafka used the standard anal language of paranoia and homosexuality which appears on projective tests in stating: "A long time ago he [Georg] had firmly made up his mind that he should not be surprised by an attack, a pounce from behind or above" (ch. 2). At the end of the story, Georg/Kafka accuses his father not only of wanting to attack him but of wanting to be attacked when Georg says: "So you've been lying in wait for me!" using this statement both literally and figuratively. Mr. Bendemann was not at all astonished when he heard this accusation and replied, "pityingly in an offhand manner: 'I suppose you wanted to say that sooner. But now it doesn't matter'" (PC, 62). In accusing Georg of betraying his Russian friend, Mr. Bendemann had also used the standard "anal" imagery of homosexuality when he remarked: "And now that you thought you'd got him down, so far down that you could set your bottom on him and sit on him and he wouldn't move, then my fine son makes up his mind to get married!" (PC, 59).

Georg, who had been overwhelmed by his tender, loving, incestuous feelings for his father, could no longer restrain himself and suddenly decided to put his father to bed. He began to undress his father, silently reproaching himself for having neglected to take care of Mr. Bendemann's dirty linens, which we mentioned were symbolic of the conflict between father and son. While he was undressing his father, Georg tried to refresh his memory by reminding him of the Russian friend's incredible stories. They were so interesting that Mr. Bendemann had even repeated them once or twice. Mr. Bendemann/Mr. Kafka, who had always misinterpreted his son's tender attentions, now became infuriated. He thought that his "young sprig" was trying to demonstrate his physical superiority over his aged father. Mr. Bendemann/Mr. Kafka had always been a worshipper of strength and power and had always had a profound contempt for the weakness of his son. While his son was carrying him to his bed as if he were a baby, Mr. Bendemann, who was a sadistic comedian, permitted Georg to delude himself that his father had really become senile. He pretended to play with Georg's watch chain, clinging firmly to it as he was being carried tenderly to his bed.

After Kafka experienced his moment of torment, he no longer had his nose "'stuck into the tide of the times'" (DI, 27). He was always late for appointments, and all of his major characters share his weakness. They are not attuned to the time of their culture and cannot trust their timepieces. Since they are all sexual deviants, they hark back to olden days when our biblical fathers strayed in the cities of the plains; or back to the time when homosexual practices existed over large areas of China and the Mediterranean countries; or they look back longingly to the time when homosexuality was an accepted way of life in Greece. "Chains" and "links" of chains represent the "chain of generations" which Kafka and his heroes must inevitably break because they are unable to marry and have children who will link them to the past and the future.

By playing with Georg's watch chain, Mr. Bendemann was symbolically trying to embarrass his son by reminding him that he would be the last of his line. Georg got a dreadful feeling (PC, 58) as he watched his father-image's symbolic act and thought his father had become an infant and was playing with his chain, just as he had played with his father's watch chain when he was a baby. As soon as Mr. Bendemann was placed on his bed, he contrived to have his son cover him up, literally, although he had already covered himself up completely. No sooner did Georg fall into this trap than Mr. Bendemann jumped out of bed setting the blankets flying. He most unjustly accused his son of wanting to cover him up (figuratively, of wanting to bury him) and screamed: "Of course I know your friend. He would have been a son after my own heart." This statement was a sheer fabrication, but since Kafka was incapable of telling an untruth, he revealed Mr. Bendemann's true feelings for his invisible son at the end of the story. At that time, Mr. Bendemann disclosed his profound distaste for his homosexual son by saying callously: "your friend is going to pieces in Russia, even three years ago he was yellow enough to be thrown away."

Mr. Bendemann raved and ranted, accusing his son of wanting to bury him and of betraying his Russian friend; then mocking Georg's susceptibility to his fiancée's blantant blandishments, he cavorted on the bed, raising his nightshirt so high that the battle scar on his right thigh became visible. Georg reacted to Mr. Bendemann's accusation that he had betrayed his Russian friend with deep despair. In a vision he saw his Russian friend's warehouse plundered and demolished. Georg suddenly realized that by alienating himself from his deviant inner self, he had sacrificed his writing career as well as his identity. His true self had been the source of his literary inspiration and had provided him with the subject matter for all of his incomprehensible stories.

From the moment the father-image began his rampage, Georg lost his mask of self-assurance and became a terrified, speechless, and senseless child. Since his mind had been vacated, he forgot every resolve he had made to protect himself from his father-image; he kept "forgetting everything." In his letter to his father, Kafka mentioned that his father had robbed him of his capacity for life, putting it into his pocket. Kafka used this image for the first time in this story. When Mr. Bendemann accused Georg of "strutting through the world, finishing deals" that Mr. Bendemann had prepared for him, and showed Georg the list of his customers which he kept in the pocket of his nightshirt, Kafka was saying symbolically that his father had robbed him of his capacity for life.

As the father-image's frenzy mounted, he leaned over the bed so that it appeared that he was about to tumble over. Georg could no longer repress his violent hatred and thought hopefully, "what if he topples and smashes himself! These words went hissing through his mind." One might have thought that the disgrace Georg had brought upon his mother's memory by making free with his fiancée, could have been eradicated by a marriage. Instead Mr. Bendemann inconsistently assumed the role of a Freudian tribal chief and threatened to sweep his son's bride away from his arms. Georg was simply incredulous when Mr. Bendemann informed him that he had become the representative of the Russian friend and could not refrain from giving vent to "You comedian!"

but he became so terrified that he bit his tongue until his knees gave way. The father-image then told Georg that his Russian friend knew everything about the engagement; he knew everything "a thousand times better" than Georg did. Georg tried to ridicule his father's magnification of the truth and replied: "Ten thousand times!" but "the words turned into deadly earnest" in his mouth. Georg/Kafka knew that Mr. Bendemann was telling the whole truth. Kafka had always believed that his unconscious had perceptions of which he was unaware; he probed into himself endlessly to become aware of these perceptions. He also knew that his father-image was telling the truth when he informed Georg that his Russian friend crumpled up his letters unopened while he carefully read Mr. Bendemann's communications. The inability of the Russian friend to communicate *directly* with Georg was the basis of the structure of this story.

The father-image concluded his tirade by informing Georg that he had been waiting for years for Georg to come to him to discuss the problem of marriage. He had concerned himself with nothing else ever since he had become the occupant of his dark cell. He asked: "Do you think I read my newspapers? Look!" and threw the ancient newspaper which he had carried to his bed at Georg. He knew every item in that newspaper by heart; he also knew that his son would never be able to marry while he remained fixated upon his father.

Mr. Bendemann then came to the point. He accused his son of being an infant, saying, "How long a time you've taken to grow up. Your mother had to die, she couldn't see the happy day." Georg confirmed his father-image's diagnosis of his psychosexual infantility by projecting his incestuous drives onto his father and accusing him of persecution, saying "So you've been lying in wait for me!" using this metaphor both literally and figuratively. Whether or not Kafka was conscious of his incestuous feelings for his father will remain an enigma. The "pitying", "offhand" reaction of Mr. Bendemann to his son's accusation seems to indicate that Kafka was aware of these drives as well as of his persecution complex.

The father's verdict was then delivered without fanfare or passion. Mr. Bendemann reiterated his basic accusation that his son was narcissistic and infantile, remarking: "So now you know what else there was in the world besides yourself! An innocent child, yes, that you were, truly, but still more truly have you been a devilish human being!" At this point, the Russian friend hypnotically propelled Georg from the room: "Georg felt himself urged from the room" and rushed madly to the bridge. The "crash with which his father fell on the bed . . . was still in his ears as he fled" (PC, 63). Georg grasped at the railings "as a starving man clutches food."

Much has been written about the last sentence of this story: "At this moment an unending stream of traffic was just going over the bridge." The German word for "traffic" also means "intercourse." Kafka told Brod that when he wrote that sentence he thought of an ejaculation. He told his young friend, Janouch, that he felt that he had exorcized a spectre in writing this story. We believe that Kafka exorcized the spectre of his boundless guilt in writing "The Judgment." Never again did his heroes go willingly to their deaths with the exception of the misogynist officer in the penal colony. It is necessary to point out that drowning for Kafka symbolized death, which was always a fulfillment; it also represented falling into a sea of aberrant sexuality. When Georg grasped the rails as "a starving man clutches food," he may have envisioned complete sexual fulfillment according to his needs.

"The Judgment" was a revelatory nightmare which told Kafka in symbolic language that marriage for him was taboo. He was much too conflicted about philistine versus bohemian standards to relinquish his security so that he could concentrate upon his writing, which was his only source of fulfillment. He was diabolical in his innocence in planning to drag another human being

deep down in his inferno. He was much too predomi-
nately homosexually oriented to be able to tolerate the
heterosexual practices he would have to engage in if he
were to get married. He was still an infant, abnormally
attached to his father and incestuously drawn to him.

Kafka had no difficulty in interpreting his nightmare.
He tried to break off his relationship with Felice Bauer,
but he was so ambivalent, so obsessed with his overwhelming need to join the circle of humanity by getting married that he became engaged to F. B. two years
later. About two months after the official engagement
ceremony, Kafka had to terminate the engagement. Like
Georg in "The Judgment," Kafka went "to pieces."

5

The Metamorphosis

Kafka identified himself with Gregor Samsa in a conversation with Gustav Janouch and confessed that he had been indiscreet in writing about the "bed bugs" in his family. He told Janouch: "Samsa is not merely Kafka, and nothing else. 'The Metamorphosis' is not a confession, although it is—in a certain sense—an indiscretion." When Janouch observed: " 'The Metamorphosis' is a terrible dream, a terrible conception," Kafka corrected his young friend, saying: "The dream reveals the reality, which conception lags behind. That is the horror of life—the terror of art" (J, 32).

Kafka had told Janouch the whole truth, ~~but, in his inimitable fashion,~~ he had contrived to make the truth incomprehensible. What Kafka was really saying was that Gregor was "not merely Kafka" as the world knew Kafka; Gregor represented the homosexual aspect of Kafka which had always been concealed from the eyes of the world. "The Metamorphosis" was not a confession because Kafka had never completely exposed himself in his true image and had no intention of removing his mask. But Gregor's metamorphosis was not a dream; it was a reality. Gregor/Kafka had literally been transformed from a man who had appeared to be heterosexual into a homosexual; therefore metaphorically he had become a vermin in the eyes of his fellowmen. The "horror" and "terror" of Kafka's life were that he feared that he, like Gregor, might one day, because of some "chance forgetting of self" (DI, 27), expose himself to the world in his true image. He would then be characterized as a vermin and would suffer the fate of Gregor.

The monstrous vermin which emerged from Gregor's room was only a metaphor. This was evidenced by the fact that Kafka refused to permit his publisher to make any graphic representation of this insect. Professor Emrich explains: "It would be meaningless to interpret Samsa, the beetle as a real beetle. Kafka himself formulated this unequivocally. When the publishing firm of Kurt Wolf planned to put out 'The Metamorphosis' and had Ottomar Starke prepare an illustration for it, Kafka wrote to the publisher on October 25, 1915, saying, 'It has . . . occurred to me that he [O. Starke] might want to draw the insect itself. Not that, please, not that! I do not wish to restrict his scope but I wish only to request it as a result of my better understanding of the story, as is natural. The insect itself cannot be drawn. It cannot be drawn even as seen from a distance' " (E, 144). That Gregor had not really been transformed into a vermin is obvious—no one had the slightest difficulty in recognizing him. However, all of Gregor's viewers were unanimous at one point: they all considered him no better than "some sort of vermin."

Gregor's "vermin" image had appeared in "Wedding Preparations in the Country." Raban (kavka), the hero of that story, wore a lady's watch "on a narrow black ribbon round his neck" (DF, 397). The watch was defective and required constant adjustment; however since Raban was attuned to the "time" of a female in his culture, a man's watch would have been patently useless. Raban had not relished the idea of going to the country to make preparations for his wedding. He indulged himself in a bizarre daydream in which he thought of leaving his inner self, which assumed the shape of a "stag beetle or a cockchafer," lying in his bed, while the clothed, empty shell of his outer self went through the motions of preparing for his impending marriage (DF, 6–7). Raban's vermin image had none of the malignancy of the loathsome "dung beetle" which emerged in "The Metamorphosis," because Raban was only pretending. He was in full control of his verminous inner image and had been able to conceal it so that no one even suspected that Raban was a vermin in men's clothing.

The homosexual bachelor in "Moment of Torment" had also characterized himself as "some sort of vermin" (DI, 23). This bachelor was filled with despair because he had to conceal himself in an ever-diminishing circle which was closing up on him. This bachelor had forecast Gregor's crucifixion when he stated that he was compelled to live as a hermit; once this compulsion was overcome by forces beyond his control, he became an insolent parasite (DI, 28).

Kafka had indicated that Gregor was a homosexual in the fourth paragraph of this story by means of his secret code. When Gregor awakened on the morning of his transformation, he felt an itching area on his belly; he "identified the itching place which was surrounded by many small white spots" and drew his leg back quickly in pain. Gregor's latent disease had erupted. His wound had broken open, and he could no longer control his incestuous and homosexual drives.

Kafka had reinforced his identification of Gregor as a homosexual when he described the dreary landscape Gregor saw from his window about a month after his "imprisonment" (PC, 94). The clock, which had marked the relentless passage of time for Gregor before he had become an outcast from the circle of humanity, had disappeared from Gregor's room. After he had decided to face the world in his true image, the "time" of the world had become meaningless for him. Space had disappeared as well as time and the ugly hospital building, which Gregor "used to execrate" for being an eyesore, "was now quite beyond his field of vision" (PC, 97). Gregor's vision had not dimmed in any way; he was able to see perfectly the grease spots (PC, 111–12) on his father's uniform from behind the open door of his cell several months after the ugly hospital building was no longer within his field of vision. Gregor had been transported from the world of ordinary men to the wastelands which provide a haven for all of Kafka's deviant characters, and he now dwelt in "a desert waste" (PC, 97).

"The Metamorphosis" is the story of Gregor, the homosexual who had suppressed his deviant sexual drives for many years and had lived a sham life because he wanted to save his family from disgrace. He had been living as a recluse by compulsion; once this compulsion had been overcome by forces beyond his control, he had awakened to find himself a parasite. Gregor had taken one step out of the circle in which he had encapsulated himself in "some distraction, some fright, some astonishment, some fatigue." Due to fatigue and stresses, reflected by his uneasy dreams, he had overslept. He had not heard the alarm that had been his inexorable warden in his former existence and had always awakened him in time for him to make the elaborate preparations he needed to mask himself so that he could face the world. Gregor had awakened to a nightmare. His disguises had permanently disappeared, and he was forced to face the world in his true image.

In his characterization of Gregor, Kafka observes himself through the eyes of his world and reports with uncompromising realism what would have happened if he removed his mask and appeared in his true image. The gallows humor of this story is the protective clowning and self-mockery of gifted humorists of all harrassed minority groups. Kafka knew that if he were to expose himself, he would be subjected to harrassment, persecution, and self-righteous brutality. Exposure would mean the loss of his job, his reputation, and his social position. His family would suffer in "the belief that they had been singled out for a misfortune such as had never happened to any of their relations or acquaintances" (PC, 113).

Kafka achieved a triumph in this story by creating a

new technique of mystification. Simply by creating a metaphor and treating it as though it were a literal fact, Kafka ensnared his readers so that it became impossible for anyone to think of Gregor except as some species of vermin. Even those exegetists who knew that Gregor was not really a beetle reacted to Gregor as if he were a noxious insect. They could not react otherwise because they were subliminally conditioned by Kafka's endless elaborations of Gregor's exhausting and exhaustive efforts to adjust himself to his new image. Kafka's contrapuntal treatment of his "vermin" image escaped the scrutiny of all of his explicators. Everyone took it for granted that Gregor had literally become "incomprehensible," that he had literally become "inhuman."

Kafka contrived to get his readers to react to Gregor as if he were a vermin by presenting him from the viewpoint of his society's bias. The reader accepted the verdict of Gregor's microcosm and took it for granted that he was loathsome, indecent, offensive, mentally sick, insolent, and an animal. No one thought of questioning the unjust law which had transformed Gregor into a monstrous vermin. Gregor had been alienated from his family and had been hypocritical in his relations with them both before and after his metamorphosis, but he loved his family and had proved his love by many years of self-sacrifice. Kafka makes it clear in this story that the dehumanized Gregor is infinitely more human and humane than his self-righteous, sadistic father; his dissembling, two-faced mother; and his playacting, obstinate sister.

When Gregor awoke on the morning of his metamorphosis, he was profoundly disturbed, but he was not unduly surprised. He knew there was nothing incredible about his transformation: "something like what had happened to him today might some day happen to the chief clerk; one really could not deny that it was possible" (PC, 75). He also knew that he was not being punished for some crime that he had committed. He had been no great hero, but he had done nothing wrong.

His only crime was that he had been ready to sacrifice his entire youth by annihilating his true self in order to save his family from disgrace.

The black humor and bitter irony in this story derives from the literal translation of Kafka's metaphor. For example, when Gregor first presented himself to the world in his true image, he stood erect in the posture of a man. After he had observed the horror on the face of the chief clerk, Gregor knew that his job was at stake and that he would literally become a parasite if he could not win over the chief clerk and persuade him to let him keep his job. Gregor's onerous job had assumed an entirely different aspect when he realized his metamorphosis was irrevocable. It had come to symbolize his passport into the circle of humanity. When he literally crawled toward the chief clerk to appeal for his job, he relinquished his human posture because he knew that henceforth he would have to grovel as a homosexual at the feet of employers to obtain a position. Tongue in cheek, Kafka described Gregor's joy when he realized that forever after he would be able to survive only by crawling before other men. Gregor could not have changed in his outer appearance because he was recognized immediately by everyone in his environment. He had the same body, the same character, and the same speech that he had had before his transformation; nevertheless he had suddenly become incomprehensible to all of humanity. An unbridgeable gap had suddenly appeared between Gregor and his fellowmen because he was a homosexual. The confusion in language between Gregor and his world mirrored the confusion in languages in the Tower of Babel, which was one of Kafka's frequently used images. Gregor understood clearly all of the people in his world; he had become incomprehensible because his culture regarded him as an animal.

The Satanic fairy-tale test which Gregor imposed upon humanity, when he decided to open the door and present himself in his true image, was perverse only because Gregor knew that it was doomed to failure. Gregor had decided to put humanity to a truly world-redeeming test because he had no other choice: his whole future depended upon it. Gregor's impassioned plea to keep his job fell on deaf ears. No sooner did the chief clerk realize that Gregor was a homosexual than he rushed to leave the apartment as if "driven by some invisible steady pressure." There was no reason why he should have remained: homosexuals were patently unemployable. The Chaplinesque humor in this episode is derived from Kafka's contrapuntal treatment of his metaphor.

The varied reactions of Gregor's world to his image epitomized the reactions of various segments of Kafka's society to the concept of a homosexual. The chief clerk was nervous, horrified, and violently disgusted. The cook was simply terrified. She fell on her knees to Mrs. Samsa begging leave to go; then after fifteen minutes she left the apartment weeping with gratitude at her dismissal. She had fervently and gratuitously promised that she would never gossip about the terrible calamity that had befallen the Samsas. The sixteen-year-old servant girl, who had the "courage" to remain, was afraid that Gregor might attack her and begged to be allowed to keep the kitchen door locked; she would open it "only on a definite summons" (PC, 101). She remained hidden behind the locked door until she was dismissed and replaced by a dowdy charwoman who came in mornings and evenings to do the heavy cleaning.

This old widow, who had survived a long, miserable, harsh life "by no means recoiled from Gregor." She had discovered him accidentally one morning. He had been terrified of her and started to rush about madly. At first she tried to wheedle him to her, "with words which apparently she took to be friendly, such as 'Come along, then, you old dung beetle!' " Gregor resented the charwoman's friendly overtures. He would have preferred it if she had been ordered to clean up his room rather than barging in on him whenever the mood struck her. This old crone opened Gregor's door daily just to take a look at him. One day, several months after his transformation,

Gregor, who had been feeling quite depressed (the rain had been falling interminably since his transformation and spring was approaching), became exasperated because of the charwoman's condescending attitude and ran at her "as if to attack her." The old lady quietly lifted up a chair; she was prepared to splatter Gregor to bits on the floor if he came any closer.

When Gregor, covered with filth and grime, trailing particles of decayed food, insolently intruded on the chamber-music concert, he was first observed by the middle lodger, who smilingly drew the attention of his friends to Gregor then carefully scrutinized him again. The reaction of the lodgers to Gregor was similar to that of the charwoman. They found him more entertaining than the concert and looked at him with curiosity and amusement. They became quite angry when Mr. Samsa frantically tried to shoo them back to their bedroom, meanwhile trying to block their view of Gregor. They retreated "with reluctance" while Mr. Samsa "kept driving them on and driving them on" to their room. The middle lodger then stopped short, stamped his foot vigorously and exclaimed: " 'I beg to announce . . . that because of the disgusting conditions prevailing in this household and family'—here he spat on the floor with emphatic brevity . . . 'I give notice on the spot.' " He threatened to withhold the money the lodgers owed for room and board and to bring "an action for damages . . . based on claims . . . that will be easily susceptible to proof."

Despite this, the boarders had no intention of leaving and were amazed when no breakfast had been prepared for them the next morning. When the middle boarder peevishly complained to the charwoman, she hushed him hastily indicating without saying a word that they should go into Gregor's room. They stood around in Gregor's room, hands inside the pockets of their shabby coats, paying their last respects to Gregor. They were taken aback when Mr. Samsa ordered them to leave instantly. With a feeble smile, the middle lodger asked, "What do you mean by that?" Only after Mr. Samsa, flanked on both sides by his wife and daughter, walked threateningly toward this crude trio, did they finally leave.

Thus had the circle of humanity passed judgment on Gregor. He had been viewed with horror, fear, loathing, disgust, condescending scorn, crude amusement, and lustful curiosity. He had lost his job, and his family had been threatened with legal harassment. It was left to the family circle to administer the *coup de grâce*.

When Gregor made his debut into society, his father, who had clenched his fist, looking fiercely at Gregor, restrained his self-righteous brutality because the chief clerk was still in the room. His fury dissolved into tears of self-pity: his family had suffered a terrible disgrace and misfortune. After the chief clerk rushed from the room, and it was clear that Gregor had lost his job, the father's only concern was to conceal his son who had brought the family to a state of utmost degradation. Stamping his foot and flourishing his stick, Gregor's father pitilessly drove him back into his room, "hissing and crying 'Shoo!' like a savage." The shouting and hissing noises sounded to Gregor "no longer like the voice of one single father"; it was the hissing, booing, and raging condemnation of all the authority figures in the universe.

Gregor had rushed back to his room but had gotten stuck fast in the door, "his flank quite bruised, horrid blotches stained the white door." His father came up behind him, "gave him a strong push which was literally a deliverance, and he flew into the room bleeding freely" (PC, 87). Gregor, who was locked into the room by his father, referred to his confinement as his "imprisonment" (PC, 94).

Mrs. Samsa acted consistently throughout the entire story; she pretended to swoon every time she caught sight of her homosexual son. When she first saw him, she "apparently" fell into a deep swoon, but, when Gregor approached her, she, "who had seemed so completely crushed," jumped up at once, shrieking for help and backing into the living room table, upsetting the coffee-pot so that the coffee poured over the carpet. Gregor, in his excitement, called out, "Mother, Mother" and the mother screamed again and fell into the arms of her husband. Gregor had become a horrendous monster in the eyes of his mother.

Kafka's interpreters have discussed the gentleness and kindliness of Gregor's mother, but there is no evidence of Mrs. Samsa's humanity toward Gregor within the context of this story. Fortunately, his sister decided to play the role of nurse and became the "expert" in the care and feeding of Gregor. If Gregor had had to rely on his parents for food, he would have starved to death (PC, 92).

Tongue in cheek, Kafka reports that Gregor's mother "began relatively soon" (it was two weeks after his trans-formation) to want to visit him, but her husband and daughter dissuaded her with cogent arguments, to which Gregor listened "very attentively and altogether ap-proved." Later, however, when Gregor heard his mother cry out: "Do let me go in to Gregor, he is my unfortunate son! Can't you understand I must go to him?" he felt that his mother should pay him a visit occasionally— perhaps once a week. His sister, who had volunteered to take care of him was only a child, and perhaps the bur-den she had undertaken had been assumed "out of child-ish thoughtlessness" (PC, 100).

The fact is that Mrs. Samsa visited her unfortunate son for the first and last time about two months after his imprisonment. She had been summoned by Gregor's sister, Grete, to help move some furniture from Gregor's room. Grete, who was the only member of the family who had made even a pretense of caring for Gregor, had decided to move a heavy chest out of Gregor's room so that he would have more space for crawling and climbing the walls. His mother walked forward quickly "with ex-clamations of joyful eagerness" but became silent when she reached the door of Gregor's room. Grete entered Gregor's room first to see if he was completely concealed;

then she called to her mother, who had been filled with "joyful eagerness" at the thought of "seeing" her son, "Come in, he's out of sight" (PC, 101). Gregor knew that his mother would stage a fainting fit if she got a glimpse of him, therefore he had hidden under the sofa and had covered himself up completely with a sheet so that he was invisible. He had yearned to see his mother but had renounced this pleasure in his gratitude for her visit.

The two women struggled hopelessly trying to push the heavy chest and had moved it to the middle of the room after a quarter of an hour's tugging. Finally his mother objected to moving it further. Because it was too heavy, it could not be removed from the room before his father's arrival; moreover, standing in the center of the room it would only hamper Gregor's movements. As an afterthought, the gentle mother, who had been unwilling to strain herself, showed her deep concern for Gregor by explaining that if they removed Gregor's furniture he would probably feel that they had relinquished all hope for his recovery and were "just leaving him coldly to himself." Mrs. Samsa left Gregor coldly to himself throughout his confinement. There was no one to dissuade her or hold her back by main force after her husband and her daughter left the apartment to go to work every morning. Mrs. Samsa remained at home doing her fine sewing, so preoccupied that she did not think of visiting Gregor. The solicitous Mrs. Samsa had told Grete that she thought it would be best to leave Gregor's room "exactly as it has always been, so that when he comes back to us he will find everything unchanged and be able all the more to forget what has happened in between." But Gregor's room did not remain unchanged. Mrs. Samsa decided to make her son's room the scrap heap for all of the filthy, superfluous things in the apartment.

Grete had inherited her father's mulishness and paid no attention to the feeble remonstrances of her mother. She could see that her mother was uncomfortable in

Gregor's room and therefore unsure of herself. Grete soon reduced her mother to silence, and the chest as well as many other articles of furniture were removed. As a matter of fact, Grete was so obstinate and self-willed that just because her mother had objected she became determined to remove not only the writing desk but also every piece of furniture in the room with the exception of the indispensable sofa. The sofa was indispensable because Grete had made it quite clear that Gregor must conceal himself completely under it before she entered the room.

Gregor soon realized that they were taking away everything he loved. He became so indignant at the loss of all of his personal possessions that he could no longer restrain himself and rushed out of his hiding place while the two women were out of his room. He did not "know what to rescue first; then . . . he was struck by the picture of the lady muffled in so much fur" (PC, 105). Gregor had not been a celibate before his metamorphosis. During his endless idle hours, he recalled "a chambermaid in one of the rural hotels, a sweet and fleeting memory" as well as "a cashier in a milliner's shop, whom he had wooed earnestly but too slowly" (PC, 114). For several nights preceding his transformation, he had been making a fretwork frame for a pinup girl enveloped in an animal skin and had proudly placed this portrait on the wall of his bedroom. Gregor quickly crawled up to the picture and "pressed himself to the glass, which was a good surface to hold on to and comforted his hot belly." Gregor, like Kafka, was not completely impervious to women's charms. He could actually enjoy bodily contact with an animallike woman if she were separated from him by a wall of glass.

Gregor's mother walked back into his room, suddenly caught sight of her son, screamed, and fell into a fainting fit. Grete shook her fist at her brother and shrieked, "Gregor!" This was the first time she had directly addressed him since his metamorphosis. Grete then rushed out of Gregor's room to get medicine to revive her swooning mother. Gregor followed close by to "advise her." When Grete saw her brother, she started in alarm and dropped a bottle of some corrosive medicine which splashed on Gregor. The bottle splintered on the floor, a piece slashing Gregor's face. Grete ran with a fistful of bottles to Gregor's room to attend to her mother, who was lying on Gregor's sofa, slamming the door shut. Gregor did not dare open the door for fear of frightening his mother and remained in the living room climbing walls in his torment.

Then the doorbell rang. Grete rushed out of the bedroom again slamming the door. Mr. Samsa had arrived. Grete, who at times found it difficult to distinguish truth from fiction, explained: "Mother has been fainting, but she's better now. Gregor's broken loose." "Just what I expected," said his father, "just what I've been telling you, but you women would never listen." Gregor's father sounded at once "angry and exultant." At last Mr. Samsa had an opportunity of giving vent to his self-righteous sadism.

In *Dearest Father*, Kafka recalled "mock" hunts during which his father would chase him around a table; he had always felt that his life was at stake. His mother would come to his rescue, rushing into his father's arms, embracing him, and pleading for her son's life. It had not taken Franz too long to become aware of his mother's duplicity. In vitriolic metaphor he described her as playing the role of "a beater during a hunt" (DF, 157). Mrs. Kafka, like Mrs. Samsa and Mrs. Bendemann, had allied themselves with their husbands, to whom they gave so much of their strength that they had nothing left to give to their sons (PC, 61).

The "angry and exultant" father advanced with "a grim visage towards Gregor. . . . But Gregor could not risk standing up to him, aware as he had been from the very first day of his new life that his father believed only the severest measures suitable for dealing with him" (PC, 108). The father chased his son around the room several times until Gregor began to grow breathless. Suddenly

Mr. Samsa picked up an apple from the dining room table and hurled it at Gregor. Gregor stopped short in panic. One apple followed another, each discharged with increasing force and speed until one landed right into his back, sinking in. "Gregor wanted to drag himself forward, as if this startling, incredible pain could be left behind him; but he felt as if nailed to the spot and flattened himself out in a complete derangement of all his senses" (PC, 109–10).

Gregor, who had been lying nailed to the spot where he had been crucified by his father, with a last conscious look saw his mother (whose clothing had been loosened by his sister during her swoon) rush into the room in her underclothes (followed by her screaming daughter) dropping her petticoats one by one as she ran to her husband embracing him and pleading for her son's life. This act is Mrs. Samsa's sole claim to humanity in regard to Gregor in this story. Unfortunately for Gregor, the rescue team of his mother and sister had arrived too late. Mr. Samsa had inflicted a fatal wound upon Gregor.

It is the opinion of this explicator that, in the episode just described, Kafka tried to convey to the reader that Mr. Samsa symbolically cast his son out of Paradise by bombarding him with apples from the tree of knowledge. We mentioned that Kafka believed that Paradise was on this earth. In one of his reflections, he stated:

Expulsion from Paradise is in its main aspect eternal: that is to say, although expulsion from Paradise is final, and life in the world unavoidable, the eternity of the process (or, expressed in temporal terms, the eternal repetition of the process) nevertheless makes it possible not only that we might remain in Paradise permanently, but that we may in fact be there permanently, no matter whether we know it here or not. (DF, 41)

Professor Emrich explains this passage as follows: "Man is thus *here* in Paradise already; he merely does

not know it. In complete reversal of the religious doc-
trine of original sin (Genesis 3:22) Kafka writes, 'We
are guilty not only because we have eaten of the tree of
knowledge but also because we have not yet eaten of
the tree of life.' " Professor Emrich then states: "man
lives constantly in 'Paradise' and would grow free of
guilt and sin if he could eat of the 'tree of life.' Kafka's
concept of guilt is not a negation nor even a denunciation of life, but it is a criticism of sham life" (E, 55).
Throughout his life, Kafka remained full of shame and
guilt because he was forced by his culture to lead a
"sham life." In "The Metamorphosis," Kafka demonstrates what would have happened to him if he had
dared to expose himself—if he had dared to eat of the
"tree of life." Only normal men, who could eat of the
tree of life with impunity, remained in Paradise.

Grete had been the only member of her family who
had asked Gregor if he were ill or if he needed anything
while he had remained behind his locked door on the
morning of his catastrophic awakening. However, when
Gregor refused to open his door and when he responded
with a round "No" to the pleas of his parents and the
threats of the chief clerk, Grete began to sob. Gregor
loved his sister, but he knew she was completely self-
centered. Using a stylistic device Kafka frequently employed to express sarcasm, Gregor explained with three
"because's" the reason for his sister's tears. She was crying because her brother refused to let the chief clerk in;
because he might therefore lose his job; and because the
chief clerk would then begin dunning the family for
their old debts (PC, 76).

At the beginning of the story, Grete had assumed a
veneer of sympathy and compassion while she childishly
played the role of nurse to Gregor, but, when she caught
sight of her homosexual brother for the first time, she
was so horrified that she slammed his door shut. Then,
ashamed of her conduct, she reopened the door and tip-
toed into the room. She brought Gregor his food and
tidied up his room, but she treated him as if he had a

foul, contagious disease. She picked up his plate with a napkin and could not bring herself to look at him.

Since Mrs. Samsa could not bear to feed Gregor, he would have starved if not for Grete's ministrations. He was extremely grateful to her but could not bear to face her revulsion. Grete acted as if Gregor had a disgusting odor—no one else in the household seems to have noticed it. When Gregor realized how disgusting he was to his sister, he worked for four hours to drape a sheet over the sofa so that he would be completely invisible. His reward was a "thankful glance from her eye" (PC, 99).

After Gregor had awakened from his swoon on the evening of the first day of his metamorphosis, he felt drawn to the door, enticed by the smell of food which had been shoved into his room by his sister. Gregor's transformation had occurred at a time when he was still a young man with a very healthy appetite. He was so hungry that he "could almost have laughed with joy" when he saw the food. But when he reached it he withdrew with repulsion (PC, 88). Like all of Kafka's deviant characters, Gregor could not tolerate human food; he needed the food of "animals." The next morning Gregor was delirious with joy. His sister had noticed that he could not eat the food of ordinary men and had brought him decayed food and smelly cheese. Ironically, Gregor reports that his sister had withdrawn immediately "with fine tact . . . and even turned the key to let him understand that he could take his ease" with his Lucullan feast. Gregor lapped up the rancid food and "sucked greedily" at the moldy cheese. The fresh food offended him and he dragged it away to some distance so that the smell of it would not spoil his appetite. The animal food Gregor's sister brought him appeased his appetite, and at first Gregor ate it with "tears of satisfaction." But Gregor, like the investigating dog, was extremely sensitive. He could not relish his food when he observed how disgusting he was to his sister.

Soon after Gregor's transformation, Grete obtained a

job as salesgirl and took courses in French and stenography in the evenings. The novelty of playing nurse had worn off; besides she was too busy to concern herself with Gregor. She pushed food into Gregor's room with her foot; anything that remained was quickly swept out with one stroke of the broom. Gregor lost his appetite when he viewed his sister's undisguised revulsion and his parents' callous unconcern. He was outraged at his family's neglect and made plans to raid the larder "to take the food that was his due" even though he knew he could not eat it. Gregor joined the ranks of Kafka's hungry heroes; soon he was starving to death. He watched with greedy eyes the three "human" lodgers gorging themselves on steaming meat and potatoes and said sadly: "I'm hungry enough, but not for that kind of food," anticipating Kafka's "Hunger Artist."

After the lodgers had sated themselves, Grete, for the first time since their misfortune, began to play her violin in the kitchen. The spokesman for the lodgers invited her to give a chamber-music concert in the living room. Gregor had had no taste for music in his previous existence; nevertheless, he had made secret plans to insure that his sister, "who loved music, unlike himself" would be sent to the Conservatorium to study. He had decided to assume this great expense, even if his parents should protest, and had planned to announce his decision to his family on Christmas day. Due to the "mishap" of his metamorphosis (PC, 121), his plans had become futile. Gregor recalled his inability to appreciate music when he heard the first notes of his sister's violin. To his profound amazement, he was enchanted with his sister's music and asked himself silently: "Was he an animal, that music had such an effect on him? He felt as if the way were opening before him to the unknown nourishment he craved."

Kafka's explicators have given lofty, abstruse, metaphysical, and theological explanations of Gregor's reaction to his sister's "music" and the "unknown nourishment" he craved. Kafka had made it abundantly clear within the context of this story that Gregor had degenerated to the nadir of animalism at the time of this concert, which was, as Heinz Politzer pointed out, a chamber-music concert "in the most ironically literal sense of the word" (P, 76). Grete may have loved music, but she obviously was not an artist. True, her family had been listening intently to her playing, but they had so little respect for her talents that they had discouraged any reference to Gregor's plan to send her to the Conservatorium to study (PC, 95).

It was *because* Gregor had become an "animal" that Grete's music had overpowered him. Gregor had become overcome with incestuous desires for his sister, and, since he was an "animal," he could not control himself. Gregor made no attempt to disguise his illicit emotions in this story. He decided to entice his sister into his room and never let her out, "his frightful appearance would become, for the first time, useful to him." No intruders would dare to enter his room. He would sit with his sister on his sofa and tell her of his plan to send her to the Conservatorium, and that, "but for his mishap," he would have announced it last Christmas. His sister would be overwhelmed with gratitude and would burst into tears, and he would then kiss her on her neck.

Kafka had written of his incestuous feelings for his sister Valli in his diary entry on September 15, 1912; "Engagement of my sister Valli. . . . Love between brother and sister—the repeating of the love between mother and father" (DI, 272–73). In "The Metamorphosis" Kafka makes it clear that Gregor was deluding himself when he hoped that his sister would never leave his room and would stay "of her own free will," just as he was deluding himself when he referred to his metamorphosis as a "mishap."

Mr. Samsa's only concern, after the middle lodger had noticed Gregor, was to keep his boarders from viewing his homosexual son. He blocked off their view of Gregor as he propelled them to their room. Then he staggered to his chair and had a fit: "The marked jerkings of his

head" became "uncontrollable." Greta was infuriated
at her brother's insolence. Passionately she pronounced
Gregor's verdict and urged her parents to permit her to
execute his sentence, saying that the family had put up
with this "creature" as far as it was humanly possible,
and now they must get rid of it or it would be the death
of all of them: "When one has to work as hard as we
do, all of us, one can't stand this continual torment at
home on top of it." Bursting into tears, she continued:
"You must try to get rid of the idea that this is Gregor.
. . . But how can it be Gregor? If this were Gregor, he
would have realized long ago that human beings can't
live with such a creature and he'd have gone away on his
own accord. . . . As it is, this creature persecutes us,
drives away our lodgers, obviously wants the whole apartment to himself and would have us all sleep in the gutter." Truth and fiction had become indistinguishable to
Grete in her passion.

Mrs. Samsa, who had been so concerned about keeping her son's room exactly as it was, so that when he
recovered from his degrading mental illness he would
forget what happened "in between," had neglected to
see that Gregor's room was cleaned. It had become in-
describably squalid; the garbage can and ash can were
deposited there. When Gregor made his third excursion
into the circle of humanity, his room was so filthy that
he could no longer clean himself as he had previously
done. He had trailed clouds of food and dust after him
onto the spotlessly clean living room floor when he went
in to attend the concert.

Mrs. Samsa was too weary to stage a fainting fit the
last time she saw Gregor alive. She sat in her chair, "her
legs stiffly outstretched and pressed together" suffering
from "sheer weariness." She could not come to her son's
defense when she heard her daughter pronounce Gregor's
death sentence. She could not plead for her son's life
because she was overcome with a fit of coughing. At first
she sat choking for lack of breath; later she coughed
"hollowly into her hand with a wild look in her eyes."

After she recovered from her asthmatic fit, she probably forgot about Gregor's death sentence.

Gregor had hardly managed to crawl back into his room when his sister hastily pushed the door shut, bolted and locked it, crying "At last!" Gregor realized that he was doomed because now there was no one to feed him. Gregor, like Georg in "The Judgment," did not blame his family. "He thought of his family with tenderness and love. The decision that he must disappear was one that he held to even more strongly than his sister, if that were possible." Gregor was not a martyr, but he could not avoid being a victim. He submitted to his fate, and in "this state of vacant and peaceful meditation he remained until the tower clock struck three in the morning." Then he breathed no more.

On his first excursion into the living room, which represented the world of the family circle and the circle of humanity, his father had given him "a strong push which was literally a deliverance and he flew far into the room, bleeding freely." On his second appearance, he had received a fatal wound when his father had bombarded him with the fruit of the tree of knowledge. His final trip had led to his death sentence.

Gregor's first ruminations on the morning of his new life were concerned with the self-destructive job he had voluntarily assumed in his former existence. His only concerns had been with train schedules, filthy beds in cheap lodging houses, poor food and irregular meals. He had been unable to make friends because he traveled day in and day out; all he had were casual acquaintances. Five years previously, Mr. Samsa's business had failed and he had fallen deeply into debt. Gregor had immediately assumed the most onerous job available, and "his success was immediately translated into good round coin" which he happily presented to his astonished family. At first this had been a time of glory for Gregor. Later, however, when he earned enough to provide his family with the luxury of a large apartment, servants, and a life of ease and comfort, the family had come to take Gregor's self-sacrifice for granted.

Before his metamorphosis, Gregor had not known that his father had been exploiting him. Mr. Samsa had slyly rescued some funds at the time of his business collapse. In addition to this capital sum, he had been able to save money monthly because of Gregor's lavish contributions. Through dividends and savings, the family assets mounted until a sufficient capital had been amassed so that the Samsas could have lived on it for almost two years. Gregor, who had inherited the counterfeit emotions of his mother, convinced himself that he felt no resentment when he learned that he had been exploited. He "rejoiced at this evidence of unexpected thrift and foresight." The news that his father had taken advantage of him was "the first cheerful information Gregor had heard since his imprisonment" (PC, 94). Gregor had been a master of dissimulation before his transformation; his character had not changed in any way after it.

The firm for which Gregor worked embodied Kafka's views on the schism between employers and employees. Kafka believed that "only mutual hatred" could "bridge the gap" between workers and bosses; he had arrived at this conviction by observing his father's business practices (DII, 73). The Chief was a typical Kafkan employer. He sat aloft behind a high desk. Since he was deaf, his employees had to get so close to speak to him that he could literally spit in their faces. All his employees were enslaved to the Chief's interests. The spineless porter's job was to report any employee who failed to arrive at the station on time. The insurance doctor's diagnoses were invariably predictable: every sick employee was a "perfectly healthy malingerer." Since the firm had assumed a personal relationship with the Samsa family by advancing funds to clear Mr. Samsa's debts, the Chief may have conferred an honor on Gregor by dispatching the chief clerk to inquire about Gregor's absence.

The chief clerk mirrored the Chief. He inspired terror by making unfounded accusations accompanied by dire threats and immediately announced that the Chief had accused Gregor of absconding with certain funds that had been entrusted to him. The chief clerk had "almost" taken the trouble to defend Gregor; he had "almost" pledged "his solemn word of honor that this could not be so," but now he regretted it. The fact that Gregor had not escaped with the firm's funds did not deter him from repeating the Chief's accusation in the presence of Gregor's family. Gregor, who had almost been driven out of his mind with anxiety because he had wasted several hours of the firm's time, was accused of malingering, dishonesty, disloyalty, and poor accomplishment.

After Gregor's transformation, the family became saddled with the responsibility of making ends meet. The asthmatic mother took in fine sewing and worked late into the night. The sister, who had led a pleasant life, sleeping long, dressing nicely, going out to some "modest entertainments and above all playing the violin" became a salesgirl and studied French and stenography at night. The father, who had deteriorated because of his sluggish, parasitic existence, momentarily became rejuvenated. He appeared resplendent in a clean, secondhand uniform with gold buttons; his tangled hair was carefully brushed and parted. He had become a bank messenger and brought breakfast to "small clerks" at the bank.

Within a very short time, Mr. Samsa reverted to his previous disheveled appearance. His smart uniform was splattered with grease; he fell asleep at the table after his evening meal and had to be wheedled to bed by the "whispering endearments" of his wife. The family ornaments, which the sister and mother had worn with pride, had to be sold. The servants had to be dismissed. An old charwoman was hired to come in mornings and evenings to do the "rough work." The lodgers, who had to be taken in to supplement the family income, appropriated the living room so that Mr. and Mrs. Samsa and Grete were confined to their bedrooms or the kitchen.

We mentioned that whenever one of Kafka's bachelors achieves a spectacular business success, putting to shame his inept old father, Kafka is evading the truth by using irony or some device of obfuscation. Kafka may have created Gregor's success story to serve as a King Lear device. It was relatively easy for Gregor to determine his family's true feelings about him when he became a burden. However, it is the belief of this explicator that Kafka intended to indicate that Gregor was sacrificing himself by paying for his family's guilt rather than for their debts. The German word *schuld* can be used interchangeably to mean *guilt* or *debt*, and Kafka used it in both senses in some of his stories. Gregor was expiating his family's guilt for having made him a homosexual. He was sacrificing his youth by leading a sham life in order to maintain his family's honor. By the time Gregor would have paid off his family's guilt, his entire youth would have been spent and his freedom would have become meaningless. The apple which Mr. Samsa had hurled at Gregor remained in his body "since no one ventured to remove it" (PC, 110). This wound, which festered and became a fatal wound, represented the psychological wound inflicted upon Kafka by his parents. Certain autobiographical details in this story seem to confirm this hypothesis. Gregor's photograph on the living room table, the portrait of a lieutenant "hand on sword . . . inviting one to respect his uniform and military bearing" was the image which Mr. Kafka would have admired and respected. In *Dearest Father*, Kafka wrote: "You encouraged me, for instance when I saluted and marched smartly, but I was no future soldier, or you encouraged me when . . . I was imitating you but nothing of this had anything to do with my future" (DF, 143–44). Kafka reproached his father for encouraging him only when Mr. Kafka's sense of self-importance was at stake and stated that he had become unsusceptible to his father's encouragement.

In "The Metamorphosis," when Gregor cannot manipulate his new body image, he thinks for a moment of calling on his father for help, but "he could not suppress a smile at the very idea of it" (PC, 74). When Gregor finally turns the key in the lock by using his jaws, only the chief clerk appreciates his superhuman efforts. " 'Just listen to that,' said the chief clerk next door; 'he's turn-

ing the key.' That was a great encouragement to Gregor."
But Gregor had wanted his family to shout encouragement, too. They should have called out, "keep going,
hold on to that key!" (PC, 80–81). Although Gregor
would have appreciated his father's encouragement, he,
like Kafka, had become unsusceptible to it and had
learned to encourage himself. When the lock finally
clicked, Gregor said to himself proudly, "so I didn't need
the locksmith" (PC, 81).

At the time he was writing this story, Kafka had felt
crushed by the endless sacrifices he had had to make to
gain the approval of his family. He had accepted responsibility for an interest in a factory, a burden he "must
have taken on in a dream." Kafka was in the throes of
an extremely creative period, deeply immersed in his
writing. He had been forced by the "whimpers" of his
mother and the "nasty looks" of his father to supervise
the factory for fourteen consecutive days because the
manager was taking a business trip. The strain of main-
taining his regular job, going to the factory afternoons,
and spending his evenings and nights in writing brought
him to the brink of suicide. He wrote a letter to Brod
telling him that he had very seriously contemplated
suicide but had decided to stay alive because "staying
alive" would "interrupt my writing less" (B, 92–93).

Brod was horrified when he received this letter and
secretly wrote to Mrs. Kafka, who made some arrange-
ment without her husband's knowledge to relieve Franz
of some of his responsibility. In a diary entry, Kafka said
that the ending of "The Metamorphosis," would have
been much better if he had not been enslaved by the
factory: "Great antipathy to 'Metamorphosis.' Unread-
able ending. Imperfect almost to its very marrow. It
would have turned out much better if I had not been
interrupted at the time by the business trip" (DII, 12).

"The Metamorphosis" is a punitive fantasy in which
Kafka depicted the "bed bugs" in his family. The parasitic family, who had exploited their self-sacrificing son,
got their comeuppance when Gregor appeared in his true

image and became a parasite. The ending is indeed imperfect and unconvincing. Most explicators stress the theme of spring and the rebirth and regeneration of the Samsa family after Gregor's death. True, Grete had blossomed into a pretty girl, and her parents would probably have no difficulty in providing her with a husband, who, in turn, would provide the Samsas with grandchildren who would link them to the chain of generations which had been broken by their sexually deviant son. But Mr. and Mrs. Samsa would have to be careful to select a young man who could provide Grete with a life of ease and luxury. Grete was a bourgeois who had worn the family ornaments with pride. She did not enjoy working too hard (PC, 124); she might even reproach her parents for "living in a gutter" after they moved from the lovely apartment which Gregor had provided for them into a smaller and cheaper apartment (PC, 132).

The asthmatic Mrs. Samsa would have to continue to take in "fine sewing," and would continue to work late into the night. She would conceal her annoyance and would look up with a "tired smile" when her disheveled husband, who had fallen asleep at the table, would wake up and say, "What a lot of sewing you're doing today." Mr. Samsa's secondhand uniform would get greasier and messier. He would soon miss the luxury of his leisurely breakfasts and would probably say: "This is a life. This is the peace and quiet of my old age" (PC, 112). The Chief would probably continue to dun the Samsas for their debts (guilt); they were enormous and would probably never be paid. There was nothing within the context of the story to indicate that the three menial jobs that the Samsa family had obtained "were all three admirable and likely to lead to better things later on" (PC, 132).

6

Kafka, the Man and the Mask

Since Kafka spent his entire lifetime deliberately concealing his homosexual orientation, it is not at all surprising that there are relatively few overt references to homosexuality in his personal letters, diaries, notebooks, or in his creative works. After he had developed his secret code, he used it not only in his creative works but also in his conversations, diaries, and letters when he felt an overpowering need to break the silence and tell the whole truth without fear of harrassment. He had discovered relatively early that when he used his code, he was as incomprehensible to his contemporaries as he was to his readers.

By use of his code, he was thus able to reveal that homosexual practices represented for him the epitome of self-fulfillment. In "Moment of Torment," he asserted obliquely that his homosexual awakening was an apotheosis; in "Investigations of a Dog," he averred that his encounter with the male hunter dog illumined him with a "sort of grandeur" (GW, 74). In this story he also declared that only the canine race is endowed with the "creative gift for music" (GW, 9), indicating symbolically that only homosexuals, who lead a dog's life in our culture, are capable of experiencing the quintessence of sexual gratification. Hiding behind his unfathomable code, he bewildered Janouch, who knew Kafka was completely tone deaf, by telling him that music (homosexual interactions) created for him "new, sub-

Kafka, the Man and the Mask 137

tler, more complicated, and therefore more dangerous pleasures" (J, 139–40); thereby expressing a typical homosexual observation. Some sociologists believe that the element of danger is a magnet for some homosexuals who at times lose all caution, risking almost certain exposure.

He had no qualms about revealing openly in his diaries, letters, and conversations with intimate friends that heterosexual relationships were for him repulsive, obscene, and horrible. He renounced his yearning for children because "children can't be begotten in any other way" (M, 137). Yet, despite his unconquerable revulsion for heterosexual interactions, he could not abandon his hopeless hope that marriage would be his salvation. Within his creative works as well as in his personal life, he looked upon women as saviors. They had the power to lead him out of the wilderness where he was impaled upon the thornbush of his deviant sexuality and bring him to the promised land of normalcy. The mere presence of a wife would provide evidence that he was living the simulacrum of the life of other men, thereby ridding him of his devastating fear of exposure and giving him a semblance of security. In "Bachelor's Ill Luck," he describes one of his numerous lonely bachelors, who lies in bed in a miserable room, suffering from some unmentioned illness (his latent disease). The bachelor yearns for a wife who will meet him on the steps and open the closed or locked doors which confront all of Kafka's bachelor-heroes. Kafka never envisioned a wife in a living room or a bedroom; for him a woman's place was on the steps or at the door.

Kafka indicated symbolically in his writings that he considered his aberrant sexuality to be a symptom of arrested psychosexual development, and that he believed that he had become fixated in a state of polymorphous-perverse sexuality because of the wound inflicted upon him by his father. In "The Judgment," he revealed his incestuous desires for his father; in a diary entry and in "The Metamorphosis," he disclosed his illicit feelings for his sister, Valli (DI, 273). A thinly veiled incestuous relationship with his mother appears in a discarded fragment in which the hero, a typical Kafka bachelor, gets into a boat with a stranger who tells him that he is his only child. In the cabin of the boat, a masculine woman with a "strong-featured face" stretches out her hand to greet him. " 'Mother?' I asked, smiling. 'If you like—' she said. 'But you're much younger than Father, aren't you?' I said. 'Yes,' she said, 'much younger, he might be my grandfather and you my husband' " (DF, 282). Photographs of Kafka's mother indicate that she was a masculine woman with a strong-featured face.

Kafka revealed openly in his diary that he was physically attracted to other men. After attending a reading by Richepin, who was sixty-two years old at that time, Kafka wrote: "I felt that Richepin had an effect upon me such as Solomon must have felt when he took young girls into his bed" (DI, 148). He was deeply attached to one of his uncles and imagined walking arm in arm with him in Paris, "pressed close to his side" (DII, 79). He had a warm friendship with Janouch, who was half his age, and, once when he saw Janouch eyeing some prostitutes, he made some comment. Janouch immediately disclaimed all interest in these women and explained: "As a matter of fact, I am interested in—in their customers." Janouch noted: "Kafka gave me a sidelong glance, looked straight ahead" (J, 181).

By protesting too much, Kafka unconsciously revealed his attraction to Max Brod in a travel journal which they wrote jointly. In this journal, he contrasted his yearning for a girl he had met on a trip with his desire for Max, who "fell short of what I needed . . . whose body I could see only in bathing without even having the faintest desire for such a spectacle" (PC, 295–96). Hall and Lind make the observation: "We know from Kafka's dreams and from his diaries of his interest in nude male bodies which both attracted and repelled him" (CHRL, 80). Kafka visited nudist colonies, but he wore trunks and was called "the man with the swimming trunks."

Kafka's obsessive concern with his body and his preoccupation with clothing have been noticed by some of his explicators. Homosexuals commonly make a large number of clothing references on the Rorschach, indicating feminine interests, or a desire to cover up their "disfigured" bodies. Hall and Lind found a marked emphasis on clothing references in Kafka's dreams, which resembled the norms for females (CHRL, 78). They also noted an emphasis on nakedness and commented,

> preoccupation with clothes can be understood as a need to conceal the naked body. It is possible also that Kafka's interest in men's clothing was a defense against jealousy or temptation or both. Yet he was drawn to a nudist colony, spent considerable time at swimming baths, and dreamed about nakedness. It is a reasonable assumption that Kafka secretly liked to look at male bodies though professing to be repelled by them. (CHRL, 85)

In a diary entry, Kafka exclaims: "Happy little B. . . . it occurs to me—but this is already forced—that toward evening he wanted to come home with me" (DII, 218). Eleven years before Kafka met happy B, he dreamt that while on a trip, he met an elegantly clothed Englishman who wore a mask over his face. The Englishman was very eager to invite Kafka to his house, and Kafka would have been delighted to accept the invitation, but a meeting could not be arranged because of Kafka's schedule. Hall and Lind observe that this dream has homosexual implications (CHRL, 81; DI, 119–20). They mention another dream in which Kafka, who had planned to go on a picnic with two friends, overslept. His friends waited outside the house for a while, then went up to his apartment and knocked at the door. While they were waiting, Kafka had dressed himself, and when his friends knocked, Kafka emerged from his room fully dressed. His friends noticed with astonishment that

> A large, ancient knight's sword with a cross-shaped handle was buried to the hilt in my back, but the

blade had been driven with such incredible precision
between my skin and flesh that it had caused no injury. Nor was there a wound at the spot on my neck
where the sword had penetrated; my friends assured
me that there was an opening large enough to admit
the blade, but dry and showing no trace of blood. And
when my friends . . . slowly, inch by inch, drew out
the sword, I did not bleed, and the opening on my
neck closed until no mark was left save a scarcely discernible slit. "Here is your sword," laughed my friends,
and gave it to me. I hefted it in my two hands; it was
a splendid weapon, Crusaders might have used it.
(DII, 110)

Hall and Lind consider this dream indicative of penis
envy and state: "Kafka acquires a large sword which may
be interpreted as compensation for a felt lack of virility"
(CHRL, 89). We suggest that it might also be interpreted as a homosexual wish fulfillment dream. Kafka
implied in his writings that he considered himself to be
a crusader for homosexual liberation. In this dream, the
emphasis is clearly placed on the fact that the sword,
which was invisible to Kafka until it was withdrawn (he
had not noticed it while he was dressing), was inserted
and removed without pain or blood. We mentioned in
our analysis of "music," that Kafka associated homosexual interactions with piercing pain. The sword which
had been driven into Kafka's back with such incredible
precision caused no pain and left no wound; "scarcely
a discernible slit" remained when it was removed. Hopefully this slit might reopen in the future so that another
sword could be inserted painlessly without blood. One
of the torn fragments found among Kafka's discarded
papers seems to substantiate our interpretation. It reads:

. . . me to pick it up. I did so and he said, "I am on
a journey, don't disturb me, open your shirt and bring
me close to your body." I did so, he took a long stride
and disappeared into me as into a house. I stretched
as though constricted, I was overcome by something

that was almost a swoon, I dropped the spade and went home. There were men sitting at the table there, . . . I at once recounted what had happened to me and, while doing so, fell down on the bench by the door; they all stood around me. An old man of proven skill was fetched from a farm nearby. (DF, 321)

This discarded fragment must have been headed for destruction. Kafka, who had been unable to persuade the executor of his estate, Max Brod, to destroy his writings, found no difficulty in prevailing upon Dora Dymant to burn some of his papers before his death.

A homoerotic reference appears in another fragment, in which Kafka describes a young director who spends whole days sitting on a chair with "some little person" on his lap, embracing him, putting his knee "on the other's knee, he requisitions his ear, to which no one else is any longer permitted to have access, and now he begins the work" (DF, 255).

Heinz Politzer and Wilhelm Emrich (P, 213; E, 361) note certain incidents in Kafka's narratives which have homoerotic overtones, citing, among others, Joseph K.'s relationship with the "shameless' bohemian artist, Titorelli, in *The Trial*. In an unfinished chapter of this unfinished novel, Joseph K. kneels beside Titorelli caressing his cheeks and "stroking his arms and cajoling him in every possible way. The painter knew quite well what K. was aiming at, but he pretended not to know and this tormented K. a little." Joseph K., "took an inordinate pleasure in prolonging the situation" (T, 308–9).

Politzer comments: "K. has made friends with the painter; in a day dream he entrusts Titorelli with the task of accompanying him back to Court. But he must pay for this assistance by suffering caresses which border on homosexuality." Politzer seems not to have noticed that Joseph K. initiated these caresses; rather than suffering, he was taking "an inordinate pleasure in prolonging the situation" (T, 308; P, 213). In *Amerika*, Mr. Pollunder "put his arm around Karl and drew him between his legs" (A, 71). Politzer observes that the Head Porter's intentions toward Karl, "whatever they may be, are couched in the language of perversity: 'Since you are here, I am going to enjoy you'" (P, 148–49). Politzer also notes that it is Karl's misfortune that he "arouses desire in both women and men" (P, 148). A number of explicators have noticed the homosexual implications of K.'s dream of the secretary, Bürgel, in *The Castle*. Bürgel is transformed into a Greek God and engages in a tussle with K. "Was it a fight at all? There was no serious obstacle, only now and then a squeak from the secretary. This Greek God squeaked like a girl being tickled" (C, 342–43).

Kafka sometimes constellates situations in which it becomes necessary for his hero to get into bed with another man. The stoker's room in *Amerika* is so tiny that Karl has no room to stand; he therefore scrambles into the stoker's bunk at his invitation. Karl becomes so enamored of the stoker that he cries when he has to leave him. The country doctor is undressed and his naked body is placed into the bed of his ailing patient. In *The Trial*, Titorelli "actually pushed the reluctant K. down deep among the bedclothes and the pillows" (T, 186).

On the journey to the Theater of Oklahoma, Karl Rossman and his friend, Giacomo, are pinched by their friendly male fellow-travellers who "could not resist giving hearty tweaks to Karl's legs or Giacomo's" (A, 297). This theater, which has been described by some of Kafka's explicators as a Utopia, was, we believe, a dead end for the misfits of society. In this "Nature Theater," singular characters who had been "actors" all their lives could relinquish the roles they had been playing and appear in their true natures. All who entered this theater were forever lost.

In "Unmasking a Confidence Trickster," Kafka portrays a coy bachelor who permits a confidence man to court him for two long hours. This bachelor was no neophyte; he knew all about confidence tricksters, how they slunk out of side streets to "meet us with outstretched hands," how persistently they refused to accept defeat, "but kept shooting glances at us that even from a distance were still compelling!" and how they tried to divert "us from going where we purposed, offered us instead a habitation in their own bosoms." It had taken this sophisticated bachelor an inordinately long time to "recognize the same old game." Evidently his mind had ceased to function for two hours in order to permit him to enjoy this flirtation (PC, 25–27).

"Resolutions" (PC, 29) depicts a bachelor who must live in a constricted circle. To avoid a "single slip," he becomes an "inert mass." He cannot be lured into taking a single unnecessary step. Throttling down "whatever ghostly life" that remains in him, he remains chaste and inviolate, defying all of his feelings.

In 1920, Kafka wrote a series of autobiographical confessions (E, 71) entitled "He." In one of the discarded passages, Kafka recalls a picture of the Thames on a Sunday. The river was filled with boats; gay young people chatted, joked, and laughed with the people in their boats and with those surrounding them. Kafka imagined himself on the banks of the river, a spectator of the scene, longing to join in with them, but he knew that he would be excluded. In order for him to be able to join in this gala, it would require so many years of preparation that ages would have passed, and it would even then "have been impossible" for him to be accepted by the merrymakers at the party. Every aspect of his personality would have had to be different, "his whole origin, upbringing and physique would have had to be different" for him to "fit in" with these people:

> And so that was how far removed he was from these holidaymakers, and yet through the very fact of being so he was, again, very near to them, and this was the more difficult thing to understand. For they were, after all, human beings like himself, nothing human could be utterly alien to them, and so if one were to probe into them, one would surely find that the *emotion*

dominating him and excluding him from the river-party was alive in them too, only with the difference that it was, of course, very far from dominating them, and merely flickered spectrally somewhere in the dark recesses of their being. [Italics added.]

My prison cell—my fortress. (DF, 380)

This passage is almost incomprehensible, unless one accepts the assumption that Kafka is harping on the theme of his homosexual orientation. He states clearly that his origin and upbringing would have had to be completely different for him to be included in this party, but he makes it clear also that he was not being excluded because of his religion, or political, or social views, but because of an *emotion* which he shared with his fellowmen. Other men were not dominated by this emotion, it "merely flickered" in their unconscious—"the dark recesses of their being." They were unconscious of their "normal" homosexual tendencies and gave vent to their warm feelings toward members of their own sex without fear or guilt in a socially accepted fashion. Kafka differed from the others because he was *dominated* by an emotion which made life meaningless for him unless he could find a comrade who existed solely for him, whose "music" existed only for him. Since he dared not surrender to this emotion, he caged himself in a prison cell which became a fortress because it saved him from social disaster.

Kafka's reluctance to publish his works continued throughout his lifetime. It is true that some of Kafka's juvenile literary creations did not measure up to his perfectionist standards, yet Kafka was not at all modest about his artistic abilities and believed that he had written some early works which he considered to be sheer perfection. It was toward the end of his life that he told Janouch why he felt so distressed when any of his works were published: " 'Personal proofs of my human weakness are printed, and even sold, because of my friends. . . . In fact, I am so corrupt and shameless that I myself co-operate in publishing these things' " (J, 26).

At about 1921, Kafka wrote a letter to Max Brod, naming him the executor of his will. This note was found in his desk by Max Brod after Kafka's death in 1924. It instructed Max to search his bookcases, home and office desks, and cupboards and bureau drawers for anything he had written and to burn his diaries, manuscripts, notebooks, letters from friends, and copies of his letters to his friends—everything was to be burned unread. He asked Brod to collect and burn the letters he had written to all of his friends; if they refused to give them to Brod, they must promise faithfully to burn them themselves. Kafka had previously written a last will, also found after his death, instructing Brod to destroy all of his writings except "The Judgment," "The Stoker," "The Metamorphosis," "In the Penal Colony," "The Hunger Artist," and "Meditations." In that will Kafka also insisted that all of his journals, manuscripts, letters, diaries, and notebooks be destroyed unread. None of his published works were ever to be reprinted. He informed Max that he would have been happy if his published works could simply disappear, but, since he could not prevent the owners of his books from keeping them, he relieved Brod of the burden of trying to collect and destroy them. This bizarre, unrealistic will was written by a lawyer who had received his doctorate in jurisprudence from the University of Prague. It is comprehensible only if one assumes that Kafka must have feared that someone might discover the truth behind the lie he was confessing after his death. Kafka was as ambivalent in his last testaments as he was in every other area of his life. He must have known that Brod, who was his greatest admirer and who prodded him to publish throughout his lifetime, would not follow these instructions, yet he may have hoped that Brod might delay publication until after Mr. Hermann Kafka's death.

While still a student at Prague University at about 1904, Kafka had written "Description of a Struggle." Two excerpts of this rambling narrative were printed, due to Max Brod's nagging insistence, in the magazine, *Hyperion* by Franz Blei in 1909. Much later, when *Hy-*

perion had to close shop because of financial difficulties, Kafka wrote an article eulogizing the editors who had erred nobly in presenting writers who dwelt on the "peripheries of literature." Kafka stated that some of the writers whose works had been published recognized that they had not been entitled to be printed; moreover they did not even want to be printed. He pointed out that some of these young writers had "natures" which kept them at a distance from the community. When their works were published, it put them in the limelight and the rest of the magazine contents made their works seem even stranger than they were (PC, 314). It is difficult to imagine who those writers were whose works were published without their approval. Writers who send their material to magazines hoping for rejections are as rare as—Kafka. Kafka's reluctance to have his works published seems to have stemmed from his fear of the exposure of his "nature" to the world.

It has been said that those of Kafka's friends who thought they knew him best knew him least. Oskar Baum, who had known Kafka almost as long as Brod and quite intimately, spent a week with him in Zürau in 1918 when Kafka was taking a rest cure for his tuberculosis. Baum mentioned that during the long winter nights which they spent in endless conversation, he learned more about Kafka in that one week than he had known about him in the previous ten years or the subsequent five. Baum remarked that perhaps some day he might write a detailed account of Kafka's state of mind at that time, which was extremely despondent and disillusioned with life (TKP, 31). Oskar Baum never revealed what he learned about Kafka during this memorable visit, but whatever he discovered could not have been of earth-shattering significance. Kafka mentioned in a letter to Milena that he had never talked with anyone "freely" during his stay at Zürau (M, 68). Bitter and indifferent to life as he seemed to Oskar Baum at that time, Kafka considered his rest cure at Zürau the most blissful period of his life until he met Dora Dymant.

Despite his undeviating honesty, Kafka was excessively cautious and evasive. He made a secret of everything and deliberately concealed from Brod, whom it would have made very happy, the fact that he was studying Hebrew. Brod, who could not bring himself to criticize Kafka in any way, became so annoyed at Kafka's pervasive secrecy that he finally gave vent to his feelings and wrote in his diary: "This making a big secret of everything. There is something very great about it, but also something evil" (B, 163). Brod had known Kafka for several years before he had any inkling that Kafka was interested in writing. Nor did he know until after Kafka's death that Kafka, who had not shown Brod any of his works until 1909, had willingly read and shown his juvenile effusions to his "mysterious first friend" (M, 116), Oskar Pollak. Kafka had met Pollak in 1902, the very year in which he met Brod, but he had never mentioned Oskar Pollak to Brod. It was only after Kafka's death when Brod read Kafka's letters to Pollak that he learned of Kafka's warm friendship with Pollak. Oskar Pollak, who left Prague in 1905 and had become a famous historian of art and architecture, had volunteered to serve in the Austrian army and was killed in September 1915, leaving a charming, witty young wife who shared his interests. Brod says that there is no mention of Oskar Pollak in Kafka's diaries, but there is an entry stating that Kafka paid a visit to Oskar Pollak's mother on November 6, 1915 (DII, 142). Kafka may have been paying a condolence call on Oskar's family. The fact is, however, that Kafka never forgot Oskar Pollak. He mentioned this "mysterious first friend" several times in his letters to Milena which were written between 1920 and 1922. Kafka may have been unconsciously attracted to Milena because she bore a marked resemblance to his first friend; by a strange coincidence, Milena's married name was also Pollak. Kafka wrote to Milena about the resemblance and promised he would tell her about this first friend, but he refrained until he met Milena at Gmund—that disastrous meeting which led to the end of their rela-

tionship. Reminiscing about this meeting in a letter to
Milena, Kafka recalled Milena lying in a meadow while
he told her about his friend, but Milena did not seem to
be listening (M, 188). Kafka must have been talking
about Oskar Pollak in his inimitable evasive fashion. It
is quite probable that Milena found him completely incomprehensible and therefore lost interest.

Herbert Tauber noted Kafka's deep emotional attachment to Oskar Pollak, saying: "The letters to Oskar
Pollak already reveal a remarkably close concentration
on this relationship with one friend only. In odd phrases
in these letters there are traits of character which hint
in advance at a later development" (FKHT, 236–37).
Although Kafka sent Oskar Pollak a bundle containing
almost all of his writings, he refrained from including
those works which he considered to be of little literary
merit and his earliest childish creations. He describes
the contents of this bundle of manuscripts in a letter
written to Oskar Pollak, dated September 6, 1903, stating specifically that he also excluded certain works which
were of such a nature that he could not show them to
anyone: "finally that which I cannot show even to you"
(FKT, 5).

Max Brod, who worshipped Kafka this side of idola-
try, became deeply disturbed at the image which emerged
when Kafka's diaries and unfinished manuscripts were
first published many years after Kafka's death. He felt
an urgent need to erase the impressions created by Kafka
in these works and to stress the image of Kafka which
had delighted him and his contemporaries. He therefore
decided to write his biography of Kafka, in which he
dwelt on Kafka's gaiety, his zest for life, his extraordinary
tact, his impeccable manners, his kindness and consider-
ation for others, his quest for artistic and spiritual perfection, his great interest in the social, religious, and
political problems of his day, his wit, and above all, his
dazzling originality.

We suggest that the two completely disparate images
of Kafka—the Kafka who existed in the memory of his
circle and the Kafka of the diaries—are in themselves an

indication of the schism which existed in Kafka's personality: he was a man divided against himself. The image Brod tried to correct and supplement was, for Kafka, his true self, which by dint of superhuman self-control, he concealed from the eyes of his world. Brod had a glimmering of this image. He knew that Kafka's "deepest wound" was his abnormal tie with his father, and recognizing Kafka's immaturity, he labeled him an "infantile," comparing him with Kleist and Proust (B, 31–34). In a letter Brod wrote to Milena, he discussed Kafka's "non-normality" (B, 234), but it seems fairly certain that Brod did not even suspect that Kafka considered himself to be a homosexual. Brod was convinced that Kafka's violent distaste for heterosexual contacts stemmed from his asceticism and from his desire to achieve spiritual perfection. Both Brod and Milena viewed Kafka through a roseate haze and insisted in placing a halo on his head.

In what Kafka called "perhaps the last" letter to Felice Bauer, he wrote:

> If I closely examine what is my ultimate aim, it turns out that I am not really striving to be good and to fulfil the demands of a Supreme Judgment, but rather very much the contrary: I strive to know the whole human and animal community, to recognize their basic predilections, desires, moral ideals, to reduce these to simple rules and as quickly as possible trim my behavior to these rules in order that I may find favor in the whole world's eyes; and, indeed (this is the inconsistency), so much favor that in the end I could openly perpetrate the iniquities within me without alienating the universal love in which I am held—the only sinner who won't be roasted. To sum up, then, my sole concern is the human tribunal which I wish to deceive, moreover, though without practicing any actual deception. (DII, 187–88)

This statement of aims was so important to Kafka that he copied it into his diary and repeated it in a letter to Brod. It is almost meaningless unless one knows that this is the statement of a "closet" homosexual who is seeking a modus operandi in life. Kafka is saying that he is not the slightest bit interested in saintliness or in meeting the demands of a Supreme Judgment. Like his investigating dog, he is striving to study the "human" community of ordinary men and the "animal" community of his colleagues, so that "as quickly as possible," he can trim his behavior to circumvent his culture's rules so that he will be able to "openly perpetrate" his "iniquities"; he will then be able to sin without being roasted. He has no compunction about deceiving the world in order to maintain the universal love in which he is held. His deception is meaningless; it is not even deception because he feels that he, like all other men, has a right to gratify himself according to his special needs, as long as he behaves ethically and indulges himself only when there is mutual desire and consent.

Kafka displayed none of the feminine traits which so many people erroneously associate with homosexuals; "externally" he was a "man like others." He engaged in noncontact sports such as swimming, rowing, and horseback riding. He believed that his psychosexual immaturity kept him young and made him appear half his age. He was delighted when he was taken for an adolescent at the age of thirty-seven. His charismatic personality inspired universal love in both men and women and an aura of greatness emanated from him. Everyone was dazzled by his originality and his wit. He frequently told the whole truth about himself by means of his code, double entendres, and puns; but his listeners, like his readers, pretended to understand him, although he left them bewildered. When he spoke about his "disease," he frequently was referring to his homosexuality, but everyone thought he was talking about his tuberculosis. He wrote Milena: "If I talk . . . about my disease, no one really believes it . . . and it is, as a matter of fact, only a joke" (M, 226). An acquaintance asked if he obtained studies of his characters in a lunatic asylum. Kafka answered: "Only in my own!" and was delighted that he had told the truth and befuddled his questioner.

Kafka's lavish use of his code words in his letters to Milena (music, balance, signposts, gravity, the road, wild animal of the forest, labyrinths, fear, inner imperfection, the Gordian knot, prisons, cages, unattainable nourishment, insomnia induced by the trumpets of the night, the way, the indestructible element in himself, etc.) made him as incomprehensible to Milena as he was to his readers. The only reader who admitted freely that he could not understand Kafka was Albert Einstein (TKP, ix). Milena was extremely intuitive and sensed that every word Kafka wrote to her was "well considered," but she frankly confessed that she could not understand his letters (M, 46). Kafka explained himself, compounding her confusion, by pointing out that those letters which seemed to her to be meaningless were the very ones in which he felt "so close to you, so tamed in my blood and taming yours, so deep in the forest, so restful in rest" (M, 46); then, in this letter of explanation, he mentioned that his restfulness was ephemeral because "the trumpets of the sleepless night are blowing again." Milena could not have been presumed to know that the "trumpets of the night" were heard only by homosexuals, this "music" was the cause of Kafka's insomnia and his nightmares.

It is our belief that Kafka never removed his mask to any member of his family or to any of his friends or acquaintances within his lifetime, yet despite this, he considered himself to be a crusader for the recognition of homosexuality. He indicated in his literary creations and in his diaries and notebooks that he was engaging in a battle against all of the obsolete laws and all the authority figures in his culture. He wrote:

> I am fighting; nobody knows this; some have an inkling of it, that cannot be avoided, but nobody knows it. I carry out my daily duties, I can be criticized for a little absent-mindedness, but not for much. Of course, everyone fights, but I fight more than others, most people fight as though they were asleep . . . but I have stepped forward and am fighting

with the most carefully considered deployment of all my forces. Why have I stepped forward out of the crowd, which, noisy as it is, in this respect is frighteningly quiet? Why have I drawn attention to myself? Why am I now on the enemy's top list? I don't know. Another life did not seem worth living. "Born soldiers" is what military history calls such people. And yet this is not so, I am not hoping for victory and I do not like fighting for its own sake. I like it solely because it is the only thing to do. (DF, 303–4)

Kafka fought alone in this battle because the "noisy crowd" that fought for political, economic, or religious goals were "frighteningly quiet" when it came to the battle which Kafka was fighting. He was on the "enemy's top list" because most of the noisy groups who were fighting for other causes would have united to destroy him if they knew why he was fighting. Kafka battled alone for ground under his feet, for a "fixed abode" within the frontiers of his culture, for air that he could breathe, for his right to exist in his true identity in his world, and to obtain the nourishment that would sustain him. He was a crusader for homosexual liberation.

Bibliography of Projective Techniques

Bergman, Martin S. "Homosexuality on the Rorschach Test." *Bulletin of the Menninger Clinic*, Vol. 9 (1945), pp. 78–83.

Brown, Fred. "An Exploratory Study of Dynamic Factors in the Content of the Rorschach Protocol." *Rorschach Research Exchange and Journal of Projective Techniques*, Vol. 17, no. 3 (1953), pp. 251–79.

Due, Floyd O.; and M. Eric Wright. "Use of Content Analysis in Rorschach Interpretations." *Rorschach Research Exchange and Journal of Projective Techniques*, Vol. 9 (1945), p. 169.

Lindner, Robert M. "Content Analysis in Rorschach Work." *Rorschach Research Exchange and Journal of Projective Techniques*, Vol. 10 (1946), pp. 121–29.

Reitzell, Jeanne Mannheim. "A Comparative Study of Hysterics, Homosexuals and Alcoholics Using Content Analysis of Rorschach Responses." *Rorschach Research Exchange and Journal of Projective Techniques*, Vol. 13, no. 2 (1949), p. 134.

Wheeler, William M. "An Analysis of Rorschach Indices of Male Homosexuality." *Rorschach Research Exchange and Journal of Projective Techniques*, Vol. 13, no. 2 (1949), pp. 97–126.

Index

Abomination: Kafka's crime an, 51; performance of musical dogs an, 64–65; Leviticus on, 66, 67

Actor: Kafka plays role of, 33; male impersonator, 33, 44

Albérès, R. M., 5

Ambivalence: Kafka epitome of, 7

Amerika: Karl Rossman in, 37; homoerotic overtones in, 141–42; mentioned, 5, 37–38

Anal language, 104–5. *See also* Homosexuality; Rorschach

Apotheosis: experienced by bachelor, 16, 17, 20; homosexual awakening of Kafka an, 136

Artist, hunger, 9, 41, 76

Asceticism: of Kafka, 149

Awakening, homosexual: of Kafka, 62; in "Investigations of a Dog," 63–64; mentioned, 13, 20

Bachelor image: of Kafka, 7

"Bachelor's Ill Luck," 137

Balance: in "First Sorrow," 45, 151. *See also* Code

Bauer, Felice: description of, 81–84; Kafka attempts to break relationship with, 88; breaks second engagement to, 110; Kafka's last letter to, 149

Baum, Oskar: reveals his lack of understanding of Kafka, 146; spends week with Kafka in Zürau, 146; mentioned, 96

Bisexuality: of Mack in *Amerika*, 38; mentioned, 22

Blei, Franz, 145

Bodily disfigurement: Kafka's theme of, 30–32. *See also* Code

Brod, Max: on "Wedding Preparations in the Country," 5; misled future expositors of Kafka, 72; on Kafka's greed for life, 80–81; attempts to involve Kafka in religion, 84; Kafka confides in, on idea of honeymoon, 88; described Kafka as a man haunted by a father-image, 93; Kafka writes to, of suicidal intentions, 134; Kafka revealed his attraction to, 138; as executor of Kafka's estate, 141; instructed by Kafka to destroy his writings, 145; annoyed at Kafka's pervasive secrecy, 147; revealed image of Kafka held by his contemporaries in his biography, 148; worshipped Kafka, 148–49; discussed Kafka's "non-normality" with Milena, 149

Castle, The: Emrich's observation of "K." of, 27–28; Kafka's code in, 45; heterosexual interactions in, 54; homoerotic overtones in, 142; mentioned, 5, 10, 59

Castration, 43–44

Chain of generations, 106